Physical Characteristics of the Yorkshire Terrier

(from the American Kennel Club breed standard)

Body: Well proportioned and very compact. The back is rather short, the back line level, with height at shoulder the same as at the rump.

Colors: Blue: Is a dark steel-blue, not a silver-blue and not mingled with fawn, bronzy or black hairs. Tan: All tan hair is darker at the roots than in the middle, shading to still lighter tan at the tips.

Tail: Docked to a medium length and carried slightly higher than the level of the back.

Coat: Quality, texture and quantity of coat are of prime importance. Hair is glossy, fine and silky in texture. Coat on the body is moderately long and perfectly straight (not wavy).

Hind legs: Straight when viewed from behind, but stifles are moderately bent when viewed from the sides. Feet are round with black toenails. Dewclaws, if any, are generally removed from the hind legs.

Yorkshire Terrier

by Rachel Keyes

Contents

KENNEL CLUB BOOKS: **YORKSHIRE TERRIER**
ISBN: 1-59378-207-1

Copyright © 1999 • **Revised American Edition: Copyright © 2003**
Kennel Club Books, Inc., 308 Main Street, Allenhurst, NJ 07711 USA
Cover Design Patented: US 6,435,559 B2 • Printed in South Korea

Photos by: Norvia Behling, Carolina Biological Supply, Liza Clancy, Doskocil, Isabelle Français, James Hayden-Yoav, James R. Hayden, RBP, Carol Ann Johnson, Bill Jonas, Dwight R. Kuhn, Dr. Dennis Kunkel, Mikki Pet Products, Alice Pantfoeder, Phototake, Jean Claude Revy, Dr. Andrew Spielman and C. James Webb.

Illustrations by Renée Low.

History of the Yorkshire Terrier

While the Industrial Revolution led most of the world toward pursuing the bigger and better, some brilliant engineers sought *smaller* and better. The Yorkshire Terrier is a remarkable man-made creation of the mid-19th century, at a time when British dog enthusiasts were crossing many types of terriers in order to develop dogs handsomely suited for their needs. In the counties of Yorkshire and Lancashire, the breed we now

The Yorkshire Terrier is a unique British creation and is counted among the world's most popular dogs.

Opposite Page: Underneath his delicate beauty and flowing blue-and-tan tresses, the Yorkie possesses true terrier pluck and personality.

The Toy Manchester Terrier may have been in the family tree of the Yorkshire Terrier.

The Maltese, with its long, flowing hair, may be a Yorkshire Terrier ancestor.

know as the Yorkshire Terrier emerged in its most recognizable form. The first shows for toy terriers in Great Britain began in 1860, and "Yorkshires" from these two textile counties were counted among the first ribbon holders.

EARLY DEVELOPMENT
Which breeds contributed to the composition of the Yorkshire Terrier, however, is still a great debate. Among the contenders are the Toy Manchester Terrier, Maltese, Skye Terrier, Dandie Dinmont Terrier and two extinct

The Skye Terrier, although significantly larger than the Yorkie, is thought to be in the breed's bloodlines, possibly contributing its unique color genes.

breeds known as the Paisley Terrier and the Clydesdale Terrier. The Paisley Terrier is described as smaller than the Skye Terrier and shorter in back, with gray coloration and a rougher coat. The Clydesdale Terrier also bore resemblance to the Skye Terrier of today, with the characteristic well-feathered prick ears, a floor-length coat in dark blue with tan markings on

the face, legs and feet, and a long body. Both the Clydesdale and the Paisley were formidable ratters, used by miners down in the shafts to kill rats that interfered with their work. The Clydesdale, Paisley and Skye Terriers receive credit for the Yorkshire Terrier's length of coat; the Maltese for coat and the diminutive size; and the Manchester for coloration. The

silken texture of the Yorkie's coat could have come from all of the longer coated dogs in the mixture, even though the Paisley and Clydesdale were usually rough-coated. Whenever silky-coated puppies occurred in a Paisley or Clydesdale litter, they were discarded until a fad for silky coats emerged. Both of these rough-coated terriers lost favor and their numbers began to diminish significantly.

The smaller Manchester Terriers that were incorporated into the early stock were fierce ratters, working side by side with the miners, killing off the vermin, with neither fear nor sympathy towards their prey. These dogs killed rats not only for employment but also for entertainment. Toward the end of the 19th century, rat-killing contests became very popular. The small black and tan terriers, with their smooth coats and fiery temperaments, proved very adept at the quick-fire killing of their ratine foes. Judged against the clock, the dogs had to kill as many rats as possible in a given time frame. Some dogs were able to slay a couple hundred rats in a mere ten-minute time frame!

PIONEERS IN ENGLAND
From Manchester, England, Peter Eden has been hailed, perhaps erroneously, as the main "manufacturer" of the Yorkshire Terrier, even before the breed acquired that name. Eden was not only an expert breeder of Pugs and Bulldogs but also a top dog show judge. His key stud dog was named Albert, who won many prizes at the shows as a young dog. Albert, the first name in The Kennel Club Stud Book as a Yorkshire Terrier, competed as a Broken-haired, Scotch and Yorkshire Terrier. Eden's influence on the breed was, without a doubt, considerable, though

The extinct Clydesdale Terrier bore a resemblance to the Skye Terrier and is evidently related to the Yorkie. This breed became absorbed into the other British terrier breeds.

The modern Yorkshire Terrier is a placid lap dog in most cases. Its ratting days are over, as the modern Yorkie is smaller than its ancestors.

GENUS *CANIS*

Dogs and wolves are members of the genus *Canis.* Wolves are known scientifically as *Canis lupus* while dogs are known as *Canis domesticus.* Dogs and wolves are known to interbreed. The term "canine" derives from the Latin-derived word *Canis.* The term "dog" has no scientific basis but has been used for thousands of years. The origin of the word "dog" has never been authoritatively ascertained.

An early 20th-century Yorkshire Terrier, Mrs. M. A. White's dog called Sensation, was considered a model for the breed.

he probably was not the true "engineer" of the Yorkshire Terrier. It is said that he purchased dogs from the men of Yorkshire and used them in his program. We are certain that he was a master breeder. Mr. Eden's dogs were among the first to possess the desirable blue silky coats marked with mahogany coloration on the head and legs, and a characteristic tuft of hair on the head to drape over the eyes. In fact, Mr. Eden's great dog Albert appears in Huddersfield Ben's pedigree many times on both sides, being twice a great-great-grandfather!

Although Mr. Eden enjoys the credit for engineering the Yorkshire breed, he does not receive more accolades than Mrs. M. A. Foster for showing and winning in the show ring. Mrs. Foster purchased Huddersfield Ben and exhibited him enthusiastically as well as the other dogs that she bred herself. Ben won nearly 100 prizes attached to Mrs. Foster's leash. Another of Mrs. Foster's top dogs was known as English Champion Ted, the winner of nearly 300 awards. Mrs. Foster promoted the breed by winning glamorously in the show ring and placing promising puppies in the hands of enthusiastic newcomers to the show scene. Mrs. Foster did for the Yorkshire Terrier breed, back in the 1860s, what we can only hope prominent breeders do for new owners today: encourage and guide new fanciers in the breed, and teach responsibility and proper care. Mrs. Foster raised her Yorkshire Terriers with the utmost care, showed the dogs in top condition and only exhibited the desirably typey dogs. Unlike many exhibitors today, who will enter the ring with a second-rate dog, Mrs. Foster

Very popular Yorkies in 1903 were Mr. C. E. Firmstone's dogs: from left to right, Mynd Damaris, Mynd Idol and The Grand Duke.

blazed trails for the Yorkshire Terrier breed. She was never seen promoting an inferior dog. Additionally, she was the first woman to be invited to judge a dog show in England. This occurred in 1889. Although her prowess in the sport was well known, it was previously unheard of for a woman to serve in this prestigious capacity.

At this point in the development of the breed, the set weight of the dogs was around 8 to 10 pounds, significantly reduced from the original size of up to 15 pounds. These smaller dogs, typical of the ones bred by Mr. Eden and Mrs. Foster, represent the trend that the breed would take over its first few decades. The Victorian

Eng. Ch. Victoria, bred by Mrs. A. Swan, was born in July 1932 and won many awards at shows in Britain.

YORKIE EXPERT AND WOMEN'S LIBBER

Prominent Yorkie breeder and exhibitor Mrs. Foster was the first woman ever to judge a dog show. The year was 1889, when the Women's Movement was well under way.

AH, POSTERITY!
The only known photograph of the great Huddersfield Ben appears in the first book on the breed, *The Yorkshire Terrier,* authored by Sam Jessop. It is a most unflattering portrait of this prepotent sire and grand little gentleman. It was taken after his death, fully mounted by a taxidermist.

Eng. Ch. Tinker of Glendinan as he appeared at The Kennel Club Show held in 1933.

sensibility for the petite and beautiful had a lasting effect on the breed, and full-grown dogs would eventually weigh in at around 2.5 to 3 pounds!

While the first dog show, in 1859, at Newcastle-on Tyne, only offered classes for sporting dogs (pointers and setters), the show at Birmingham the following year included toy terriers. Birmingham, by the way, is the present location of England's most prestigious and oldest show, the Crufts Dog Show. "Yorkshires," though not by name, were present at the show. "Scotch" or "Broken-haired Terriers" were the names usually applied to dogs in these toy terrier classes. The ancestors of our Cairns, Scotties, Dandie Dinmonts and Skyes were likely included in these classes. Not until the Yorkshire Terrier Club became established in 1898 did the dogs compete

under the uniform appellation "Yorkshire Terrier."

The term "toy terrier" would seem to have initiated a veritable scandal for those interested in the Yorkshire Terrier. Since many of the Yorkie's contributing forefathers were rough-and-tumble, rough-coated terriers, certain fanciers preferred the Yorkshire to be a true working terrier. The other camp, guided by their Victorian ideals, sought a diminutive silky-coated dog, suitable for warming your lap instead of exterminating the vermin in your stables. This camp desired a toy dog, not a terrier! Some dedicated Yorkshiremen, well known as industrious and clever dogmen, wanted a competent rat-killer that was also attractive. Thus, the first batch of "Yorkshire pudding" was whipped up, crossing the talented and fearless Broken-haired terriers with the smaller and somewhat unusual Clydes-dale, no less undaunted in the rat pits. There is no doubt that it took many additions to the recipe, at least six different terrier types, to finally reach the desirable, dutiful Yorkshire Terrier—a diminutive charmer in blue and bronze, capable of the task at hand. It would seem that the long coat of the York-shire Terrier would interfere with the task of killing rats underground. Not necessarily, as some historians purport that the long coat gave the miners something to grab onto to pull the dog out of the ground. As the Yorkshire Terrier developed, the controversy between terrier and toy faded, since many workers decided that the York-shire was an excellent worker, despite its fancy appearance. Today the breed is still the hearty little terrier, though his smaller size and sweet person-able character have become his hallmark claims to fame. The Yorkshire's ability to warm his owner's home, in modern times, certainly outclasses his ability to keep it vermin-free.

The Yorkshire Terrier was among the first breeds recog-nized by the newly formed Kennel Club in 1873. A quarter century passed, however, before the breed's official standard was drafted. Established in 1898, England's Yorkshire Terrier Club formed in order to write a standard for the breed.

THE YORKSHIRE TERRIER IN THE U.S.
The first blue and tan to be heralded in the land of the red, white and blue was Belle, a bitch whelped in 1877, owned by Mr. A. E. Godeffroy. Belle was registered before the Amer-ican Kennel Club (AKC) was formed, in a ledger belonging to A. N. Rouse. Two other early imports, among the first in the AKC Stud Book, were known as Jim and Rose, both derived from

MURDER BY THE DOZEN
In the rat pits, Yorkies were used to kill rats against the clock. Among the great Yorkshire Terriers who excelled in the rat contests was Huddersfield Ben, one of the most important early Yorkshire Terriers, the sire of many champions. He died in 1871. Ben was bred by W. Eastwood of Huddersfield and later sold to Mrs. M. A. Foster of Bradford.

Scottish breeding. They were owned by J. A. Nickerson and R. R. Bushell of Boston, Massachusetts.

Around 1900, George Stedman Thomas, who had imported four of the original Yorkshire Terriers to the States, joined forces with Charles N. Symonds to promote the breed in the U.S. It is Thomas who is credited for championing the Yorkie in the breed ring, and he exhibited his dogs at Westminster Kennel Club for over 25 years. He and his wife won many first prizes during this period and really put the little Yorkie on the show-dog map in the U.S.

Another noteworthy pioneer of the breed was Goldie Stone, who began her well-respected Petite Kennels in 1929. She

WHAT'S IN A NAME?
The word *terrier* in Yorkshire Terrier has real meaning. The early members of the breed were terrific ratters. Admittedly these early Yorkies weighed in at around 14 pounds, compared to the wee 5-pound dogs we cherish today.

continued to produce show winners for over 50 years, including many Group-winning and Best in Show dogs. Along with Goldie Stone were a number of other great pioneers from the 1920s, including John Shipp (Rochdale), Mrs. Emanuel Batterby (Hunslet), Anna Radcliffe, William Thompson, Mrs. W. A. Beck, E. Proctor, Julie McGoldbrick, Mrs. August Kohlmeyer and Andrew Patterson (Columbine).

The 1930s was marked by many significant wins for Yorkies in the ring. The year 1933 began a remarkable trend for the breed at the Westminster Show. Earl Byng placed fourth in the Group at Westminster, and, in 1934, Ch. Haslingden Dandy Dinty placed third. Both of these dogs were owned by Andrew Patterson. For the next three years, Yorkies placed in the Group: Ch. Rochdale Queen of the Toys, owned by John Shipp, in 1935; and Ch. Bobbie B. III, owned by Samuel Baxter, in 1936 and 1937. After a string of impressive wins, finally in 1939, a Yorkie won the Group: Ch. Miss Wynsum, owned by Arthur Mills, the owner of the Millbarry Kennels, easily the most prominent Yorkie breeders of the 1930s. Many decades would pass before a Yorkie would win Best in Show at Westminster.

WKC

The Westminster Kennel Club Dog Show, held annually since 1877, is the oldest continuous dog show in the world. This unique American event, second only to the Kentucky Derby as oldest sporting event in the U.S., attracts 2,500 dogs each year at Madison Square Garden in New York City. Only one Yorkshire Terrier has ever won Westminster, and it took the breed over 100 years to do so: Ch. Cede Higgins, owned by Barbara and Charles Switzer, claimed top honors in 1978.

The breed rose in popularity in the 1940s, and there were many breeders of note who produced top-winning Yorkies. Among the leaders were Kay Finch (Crown Crest), Aileen Markley Martello (Stirkean, from Goldie Stone), Theron and Bette Trudgian (Trudg-Inn), Mrs. Stanley E. Ferguson, Myrtle Durgin, Pearl Johnson, Stella Sally Myers and Ruby Erickson.

The 1950s saw American breeders in greater numbers than ever as well as the founding of the Yorkshire Terrier Club of America in 1951, when a group of ten influential Yorkie fanciers from around the country met at the California home of Kay Finch. The following year, the club held its first sanctioned match in Los Angeles, with over 50 Yorkies entered. The club was accepted by the AKC in 1958 and the breed standard, based largely on the British standard, was accepted by 1966. That standard has remained in effect, with minor changes, until the present day. The club has grown to include over 500 members with over 20 regional clubs around the country. *The Yorkie Express*, a quarterly newsletter, is distributed by the club.

The Yorkie's stronghold in the States began to firm up in the 1950s and the following

WHO'S AFRAID OF THE BIG BAD MOUSE!
WHO'S AFRAID OF THE BIG BAD MOUSE! If you have ever known a Yorkshire Terrier, there is little doubt that this toy dog knows well his fearless, animated ancestors. While he is considerably too small to take on a full-grown rat (that could easily outweigh him), he is more than willing to do battle with a mouse.

decades, and the legions of breeders are too many to name in this brief chapter. It goes without saying that the Yorkshire Terrier in the U.S.,

An Irish Yorkshire Terrier named Little Pickwick was owned by Miss Sally Logan of Belfast. At the 1931 Navan Dog Show, held in County Meath, Ireland, it won First Any Variety Toy, First Any Variety Terrier, First Yorkshire Terrier and Best Yorkshire in Show.

through the efforts of the parent club and thousands of dedicated breeders, exhibitors and judges, has become the nation's number-one Toy breed. The American Kennel Club registers around 40,000 Yorkie puppies each year out of about 25,000 litters! The quality of the breed in the States continues to be high and the breed is in the competent hands of the many responsible fanciers who devote their worlds to the irresistible Yorkshire Terrier.

One of Mrs. Swan's best examples (1933) of a Yorkshire Terrier.

According to *Hutchinson's Encyclopedia*, published in the 1930s, "A Yorkshire Terrier's coat needs cultivating with extreme care, especially the full beard and moustaches, which should never be left untied. Coats that trail the ground should be rolled in paper and securely tied to allow the dog maximum freedom of movement."

Characteristics of the Yorkshire Terrier

THE JOY OF LOVING A YORKIE
Who can resist the charms of a Yorkshire Terrier? What could shake the blues from your lonely evening more readily than a blue and tan toy terrier? It would appear that most anyone inclined to own a Yorkshire Terrier should do so! There are so many gigantic advantages wrapped up in this smallest of toy terriers.

Given the tiny size of the breed, the Yorkshire does not impose upon your space. You do not need a palatial estate with a top-security fence. You do not need a large home to provide ample exercise for the dog indoors. You do not need to stress your budget to afford to feed the dog. You do not need to purchase expensive equipment to train, house and otherwise accommodate the Yorkshire Terrier.

You do need to open your heart to this 3-pound wonder and learn to give yourself freely and without reservation to another living creature. The Yorkshire Terrier welcomes everyone into his world. He is a trusting soul, who shares his affectionate ways with anyone kind and good-humored enough to spend time with him. Yorkies like people most of all. While they get along with most other dogs, they are not clannish or selfish. Owners are advised to supervise the introduction of their Yorkies to larger dogs. Even though your Yorkie will not be afraid of a larger dog, such as a Doberman Pinscher or German Shepherd, the larger dog may not realize his own strength. Many Yorkies have been harmed by larger dogs that playfully mouthed them or pawed down at them. Once the larger dog realizes that the Yorkshire Terrier is a member of his canine clan, he

(Opposite page) Yorkshire Terriers are so popular now because they are beautiful, small and intelligent. They are like living dolls...but unlike a doll, a dog needs proper care and attention.

A pet Yorkie can be kept in a clipped coat, greatly reducing the amount of coat care and grooming.

will want to "talk dog" with the Yorkie, unaware of the Yorkie's genteel status.

Although not the size of a guard dog, the Yorkshire Terrier is most protective of his home and people. He still possesses all the fire of his terrier ancestors—he is fearless beyond his size. A Yorkshire Terrier, whose temper is incited, will make quite a display of spit and attitude when protecting his owner's property, car or home. Yorkies have the memory of elephants! Once you cross a Yorkie and he brands you a foe, he will never forget your transgression.

For the most part, Yorkies love to have great fun. They are

A MATTER OF SIZE!
While the Yorkie may be smaller than what the world commonly thinks of as a dog, he is nonetheless completely dog. The Yorkie thinks and acts like every other canine. He interacts with other dogs the same as any other dog. Other dogs react to him in a thoroughly canine way. Dogs do not perceive size the way humans perceive size. A pint-sized Yorkshire Terrier does not look upon a Basset Hound, Great Dane or Greyhound in awe of its greater size. For the Yorkie's size, he is a giant—a full-size ambassador of goodwill, confident and regal.

Though Yorkies are not truly watchdogs, they are extremely protective of their homes and human families.

not vindictive, despite their serious ways in serious times. As with most other toy dogs, play is a way of life! Simple games, such as rolling a ball, chasing a string, fetching a bone, etc., make the Yorkie a happy pal to have about. His extroverted personality, coupled with his playful air, make him an ideal choice for young and old alike. Jumping about the furniture and leaping after imaginary mice and other foes, the Yorkshire Terrier can entertain even the most reserved of guests.

Children and the Yorkie are natural companions. Given the petite size of the Yorkie, caution

is in order. Most breeders recommend that larger Yorkies (even in excess of the 7-pound limit) be selected for families with children. Since young people tend to be pretty rough on their toys (and toy dogs), children must be taught that the Yorkie is a fragile living creature. This is not a doll that can be tossed about with abandon, though admittedly the

Children and Yorkies are made to order for each other, though children must be instructed that the small Yorkie is a delicate living creature that must be treated with care.

Yorkie is as adorable and as precious! The Yorkshire Terriers can be injured by excitable children who poke at their eyes or tear a ligament or break a leg by tossing or dropping the young dog. Yorkies have much to teach children in terms of care, trust and mutual affection. When properly instructed and supervised, this is a marvelous pairing.

The elderly also adore Yorkshire Terriers. Their entertaining antics and gentle ways make them suitable for the housebound and those less likely to take their dogs jogging on the oceanfront. Yorkies can receive ample exercise indoors, with an occasional romp through the yard. They are ideal for apartment dwellers or others living in small townhouses without much access to the outdoors.

When the Yorkshire Terrier is given access to the great outdoors, however, he takes to it with zeal. He is a terrier, after all, and the word "terrier" derives from the Latin word for earth. Yorkies love to play in the grass. They are talented diggers, you can be certain. The breed welcomes all the sporting games of the larger terriers. Although the Yorkie has neither the poundage of the Dandie Dinmont nor the legginess of the Airedale, some of the game and pluck of his terrier ancestors still race through his blue arteries.

Most Yorkshire Terrier owners admit that being possessed by a Yorkshire Terrier is infectious. Yorkies are not great family dogs, they are family! Owners consider their Yorkies to be a part of the family,

THE DELECTABLE, COLLECTABLE YORKSHIRE TERRIER

Since the Yorkie does not require much space in one's home, owners have a tendency to "stock up" on them. It is very common for Yorkie enthusiasts to adopt two, three or even a dozen Yorkies! The love and companionship that a single Yorkie can bring to an owner is multiplied and compounded daily with a whole collection of blue and tan babies!

Being possessed by a Yorkie is one of life's inexplicable joys.

like any other child in the household. Given the Yorkie's size and the giant size of his heart and character, it is no surprise that owners depend on their Yorkies for companionship and affection. Thus, many true Yorkie fanciers build a whole family of Yorkies. While most dog breeders will discuss their kennel plans, it is rare to hear a Yorkie breeder talk about a "kennel." The Yorkshire is a home buddy, always living amid the family, totally immersed

It's easy to want to spoil your Yorkie, but don't give in! They require polite, kind attention without your accommodating their every wish.

and involved in the family's day-to-day routine.

Yorkies operate on the family's schedule. They instinctively know who comes home first, and, likewise, they know when someone is late or missing. This family dog cannot sleep if one of his beloved is still not home where he or she belongs. While the Yorkie counts his master or mistress first (like all dogs, the one who feeds and cares for them receives special consideration), every member of the family is regarded in the highest esteem.

A word of caution to the overzealous Yorkie lover: You must resist your primal urge to spoil your Yorkshire Terrier beyond reason. Any overly pampered dog can become difficult to live with. Considering this toy terrier's spirit and determination, once a Yorkie thinks he has his way in all matters of the household, he may become less of a joy to have around. By nature, the Yorkie is not a selfish, greedy dog; he is not a stingy eater and does not gorge himself; he does not hide his toys from his playmates and is quite happy to share his things. Once your obsession has spoiled this delightful personality, your Yorkie may not be the generous, open-hearted angel you fell in love with.

Be careful. Many "Yorkie-aholics," among whom the author

The Yorkie is a lot of personality in a little dog.

might be counted, have embarrassing stories about the extents to which they go to spoil their adorable little friends. Although this fancier has never resorted to anything like this, I have heard of Yorkie owners who have purchased cradles and highchairs for their Yorkies; who visit the butcher daily to furnish top-grade sirloin; who have cancelled vacation plans if the six Yorkies were not invited; who have knitted and crocheted sweaters and hats for their dogs; and who have given up highly successful careers in the business world to stay home with their Yorkies (and freelance write about her favorite subject?!).

If you find yourself falling into any of the above categories, then you will fit in well with the wonderfully dedicated, delicately balanced world of Yorkshire Terrier ownership. Welcome!

BREED-SPECIFIC HEALTH CONCERNS OF THE YORKSHIRE TERRIER

Your Yorkie's eyes are not only a good indication of his affection and devotion for you, his owner, but also an excellent way of evaluating the dog's health. As in all dogs, the eyes should be clear and bright, a general sign of good health and intelligence. Look for any cloudiness or opacity in the eyes of your dog; this could indicate a problem to bring to your veterinarian's attention. With the Yorkshire Terrier, however, the breed is prone to some hereditary eye conditions. Among these conditions, the most common are cataracts, progressive retinal atrophy, keratoconjunctivitis sicca, and ulcerative keratitis.

Yorkies tend to develop cataracts after three years of age, most frequently between three and six years. Fortunately, veterinary advances make it possible for

Yorkie owners should pay special attention to their dogs' eyes. Any sign of cloudiness in the eye is reason to visit the vet.

successful cataract surgery to take place. As in humans, the cataracts can be removed by a trained ophthalmologist.

Progressive retinal atrophy, abbreviated PRA, causes blindness in affected dogs. Commonly, the Yorkshire Terrier is struck by PRA in the later years, usually around 8 years of age, though it can be as early as 5 and as late as 12. As the name describes, the deterioration of the retina worsens over time. Affected dogs experience limitations in their sight, but since Yorkies are very adaptive, the owner may not notice that the dog's sight is failing. Usually, PRA has become rather severe by the time the owner is aware that the dog is affected.

Keratoconjunctivitis sicca is abbreviated KCS and is more commonly called "dry eye." The "dry eye" condition results from

Make sure your Yorkie's eyes are clear and bright, without any sign of mucus.

the lacrimal glands' failure to produce tears in the eye. The cornea suffers from lack of "wetness," and these dry areas cause damage to the eye. Mucus accumulation around the eyes indicates to the owner that there is a problem with the eye. Treatment is available, which includes antibiotics and other drugs. In unusual cases, surgery can correct the condition. Like PRA, KCS is hereditary and affected dogs should not be bred.

The fourth eye condition

Your vet should be able to diagnose a problem at its onset and keep your Yorkie as healthy as he is beautiful.

affecting the Yorkie, ulcerative keratitis, also affects the cornea. Infection and ulceration (formation of ulcers) on the cornea are caused by the dog's hair's irritating its eyes. Owners may notice their Yorkies blinking excessively and pawing at their eyes from discomfort, and a watery appearance to the eye. This is not a hereditary condition but merely a result of the Yorkshire Terrier's prominent eyes. The condition

CONTACT LENSES FOR YOUR YORKIE!
Does your Yorkshire Terrier need contact lenses?! Yes, some Yorkies affected with severe cases of ulcerative keratitis are fitted with contact lenses. Unlike in humans, these lenses do not correct the vision, but they do protect the dogs' lenses from any irritating fur, which causes the ulcers on the eyes.

Yorkies have prominent eyes that are susceptible to irritation. Keeping the dog's eye area free of excess hair can help prevent a problem.

can be treated with antibiotics and special applications.

Two orthopedic conditions that commonly affect toy dogs and other small breeds are Legg-Calve-Perthes disease and patellar luxation. Commonly seen in young Yorkies, Legg-Calve-Perthes has a high incidence in the breed. The disease causes lameness in the hip joint, resulting from the collapsing of the femoral head of the leg. Very frequently, in eight or nine out of ten cases, only one leg is affected. It is likely hereditary, though veterinary research is not conclusive. Patellar luxation, in layperson's terms, means a "slipped kneecap." Although it is hereditary, it is not usually a serious problem. Cases vary greatly depending on the laxity of the patella. In young dogs, surgery is commonly recommended before the condition causes arthritis.

Von Willebrand's disease (vWD), a congenital bleeding

HONKING: A SIGNAL

Honking, hacking Yorkies should signal concern in owners. A honking cough from a Yorkshire Terrier, particularly around seven or eight years of age, accompanied by obesity, often indicates a collapsed trachea. The honking attacks are aggravated by stress. The condition can be treated, but weight loss and stress management are mandatory.

disorder, is seen in many breeds of dog. Unfortunately, the disease is becoming of increasing importance to the Yorkshire Terrier. Breeders and vets have noted a large number of cases in recent times, particularly in dogs

Yorkies and children seem to see eye to eye about most of life's dilemmas.

The present and future health of your Yorkshire Terrier depends upon your selection of a good vet, keeping current with veterinary visits, and being diligent about the dog's everyday health care.

over five years of age. Not all dogs with vWD are diagnosed, depending on the level of clotting. Some dogs are not diagnosed until a problem presents itself in surgery (spaying and neutering procedures most commonly). Depending on the level of clotting factor, the dog may or may not be badly affected. No Yorkshire Terrier with vWD should be included in a breeder's program.

In all, the Yorkshire Terrier is a healthy, adaptable dog. Owners are well advised to investigate each of the aforementioned disorders and to discuss them with the vet. The better informed an owner is, the longer will be the life of his Yorkshire Terrier.

Your Yorkie depends upon you for food, shelter, affection and health care. If you are unable or unwilling to supply these essentials, you should reconsider bringing a dog into your life.

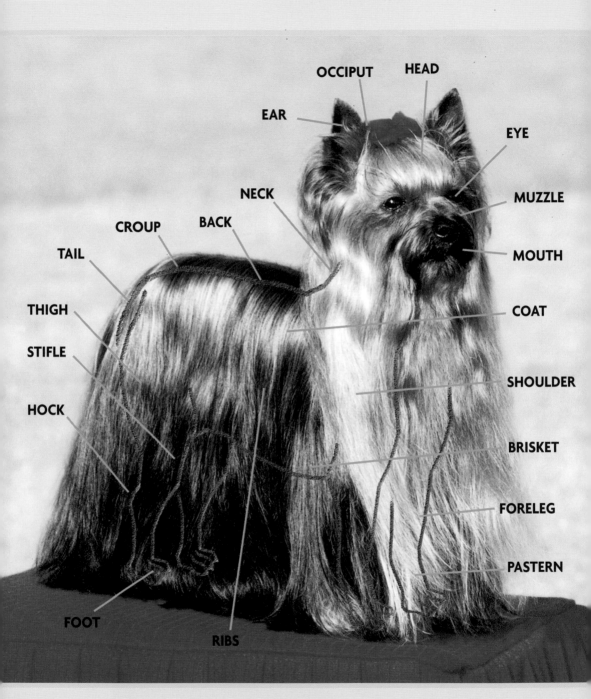

OCCIPUT

HEAD

EAR

EYE

NECK

MUZZLE

CROUP

BACK

MOUTH

TAIL

THIGH

COAT

STIFLE

SHOULDER

HOCK

BRISKET

FORELEG

PASTERN

FOOT

RIBS

Breed Standard for the Yorkshire Terrier

The breed standard for the Yorkshire Terrier, originally drafted by the Yorkshire Terrier Club of America and accepted by the American Kennel Club, is the written description of the perfect representative of the breed. Breeders and show judges use this standard to determine which Yorkshire Terriers are suitable for breeding and winning ribbons at dog shows. The standard presents a dog that possesses the key features that every Yorkie should possess, not just show and breeding animals. Pet owners are wise to read and understand the requirements set herein so that they are better informed when it comes to selecting a typical Yorkie, a dog that possesses all the esthetic and temperamental qualities that attracted them to the breed in the first place.

THE AMERICAN KENNEL CLUB STANDARD FOR THE YORKSHIRE TERRIER

General Appearance: That of a long-haired toy terrier whose blue and tan coat is parted on the face and from the base of the skull to the end of the tail and hangs evenly and quite straight down each side of body. The body is neat, compact and well proportioned. The dog's high head carriage and confident manner should give the appearance of vigor and self-importance.

Head: Small and rather flat on top, the skull not too prominent or round, the muzzle not too long, with the bite neither undershot nor overshot and teeth sound. Either scissors bite or level bite is accept-

This is what a champion Yorkshire Terrier looks like when groomed for show.

The body is long coated, with hair hanging straight and evenly down each side.

The head is characterized by small, V-shaped ears, held erect and covered with hair.

The ears must not be too far apart or held incorrectly, which will spoil the desired expression.

The muzzle must never be too long (incorrect muzzle shown in left illustration); the nose is black.

The mouth must exhibit a perfect scissors bite, with teeth well placed in even jaws.

toenails. Dewclaws, if any, are generally removed from the hind legs. Dewclaws on the forelegs may be removed.

Tail: Docked to a medium length and carried slightly higher than the level of the back.

Coat: Quality, texture and quantity of coat are of prime importance. Hair is glossy, fine and silky in texture. Coat on the body is moderately long and perfectly straight (not wavy). It may be trimmed to floor length to give ease of movement and a neater appearance, if desired. The fall on the head is long, tied with one bow in center of head or parted in the middle and

With a mustache touching the ground, this magnificent specimen has the silken hair of rich golden tan on the fall of the head.

The coat of the young Yorkshire Terrier will develop into the long silky adult coat as the puppy grows.

able. The nose is black. Eyes are medium in size and not too prominent; dark in color and sparkling with a sharp, intelligent expression. Eye rims are dark. Ears are small, V-shaped, carried erect and set not too far apart.

Body: Well proportioned and very compact. The back is rather short, the back line level, with height at shoulder the same as at the rump.

Legs and Feet: Forelegs should be straight, elbows neither in nor out. Hind legs straight when viewed from behind, but stifles are moderately bent when viewed from the sides. Feet are round with black

This lovely champion clearly shows the striking difference between the dark steel blue on the rear portion of the dog and the golden tan hairs on the headfall.

CARING IS THE KEY

The behavior and personality of your dog will reflect your care and training more than any breed characteristics or indications. Remember that these dogs require a purposeful existence and plan your relationship around activities that serve this most basic and important need. All the good potential of the breed will necessarily follow.

tied with two bows. Hair on muzzle is very long. Hair should be trimmed short on tips of ears and may be trimmed on feet to give them a neat appearance.

Colors: Puppies are born black and tan and are normally darker in body color, showing an intermingling of black hair in the tan until they are matured. Color of hair on body and richness of tan on head and legs are of prime importance in adult dogs, to which the following color requirements apply: *Blue:* Is a dark steel-blue, not a silver-blue and not mingled with fawn, bronzy or black hairs. *Tan:* All tan hair is darker at the roots than in the middle, shading to still lighter tan at the tips. There should be no sooty or black hair intermingled with any of the

tan. *Color on Body:* The blue extends over the body from back of neck to root of tail. Hair on tail is a darker blue, especially at end of tail. *Headfall*: A rich golden tan, deeper in color at sides of head, at ear roots and on the muzzle, with ears a deep rich tan. Tan color should not extend down on back of neck. *Chest and Legs:* A bright, rich tan, not extending above the elbow on the forelegs nor above the stifle on the hind legs.

Weight: Must not exceed seven pounds.

Approved April 12, 1966.

Always confident, the Yorkshire Terrier should appear neat, compact and well proportioned.

The Yorkshire Terrier acquisition is more an adoption than a purchase. Are you prepared to become a parent to the new Yorkie baby?

Your Puppy Yorkshire Terrier

OWNER CONSIDERATIONS

Owning a Yorkshire Terrier is a giant commitment. The responsibility of dog ownership, even a dog as small and unimposing as a Yorkshire Terrier, must be taken seriously. The dog must be considered in every aspect of the owner's lifestyle. Dogs require attention, not to mention food, water, walks, veterinary care and lots more. Even though a Yorkshire Terrier will not require as much outside time as a Golden Retriever, for example, he will enjoy a daily walk plus require frequent breaks to be in the yard

Acquiring any living pet requires a commitment on your part. This is especially true of a tiny Yorkshire Terrier, who will rely upon you to safeguard his well-being.

to relieve himself. Long weekends and vacations must be planned with the dog in mind. Although the Yorkshire Terrier may be a bit smaller than the family cat, he requires much more commitment than a cat, who is mostly content to look after itself.

The Yorkshire Terrier thrives

SPOILING THE YORKIE

Since we know that Yorkies can easily be spoiled, it is wise to advise owners about the dangers of "spoiling their Yorkie's appetite." The caloric requirements of a toy dog is about 500 calories per day, so it only takes about two or three treats to throw your Yorkie off his diet. A Yorkie cannot be expected to eat his full day's ration if he has already consumed 300 calories in treats. Spare the cookies and save them for special occasions and training sessions.

It is not too difficult to imagine that owning two Yorkies is at least twice the pleasure of owning one!

on the time spent with his special people. There is no breed that depends on his human family as much as the Yorkshire Terrier. Committing yourself to the care of such a giving, loving animal is akin to accepting the responsibility of a child. Although the Yorkie will not grow up and move out of your home when he is 18, he will look up to you as a parent and depend on you for food, shelter and affection.

Most Yorkshire Terrier enthusiasts keep the breed as a home companion and not as a show dog. Although the Yorkshire Terrier excels in the show ring, thriving on the attention and the pageantry, most Yorkies never have the opportunity to strut their glamorous selves for the judges and the crowd. Whether you are seeking a show dog or a home companion, there are a number of considerations to keep in mind when acquiring a Yorkie.

ACQUIRING A PUPPY

Potential owners should set out to purchase the best Yorkshire Terrier that they can possibly afford. The safest method of obtaining your puppy is to seek out a local reputable breeder. This is suggested even if you are not looking for a show specimen. The novice breeders and pet owners who advertise at attractive prices in the local newspa-

pers are probably kind enough towards their dogs, but perhaps do not have the expertise or facilities required to successfully raise these animals. These pet puppies are frequently badly weaned and left with their mother too long without any supplemental feeding. This lack of proper feeding can cause indigestion, rickets, weak bones, poor

PEDIGREE VS. REGISTRATION CERTIFICATE

Too often new owners are confused between these two important documents. Your puppy's pedigree, essentially a family tree, is a written record of a dog's genealogy of three generations or more. The pedigree will show you the names as well as performance titles of all the dogs in your pup's background. Your breeder must provide you with a registration application, with his part properly filled out. You must complete the application and send it to the AKC with the proper fee. Every puppy must come from a litter that has been AKC-registered by the breeder, born in the US and from sire and dam that are also registered with the AKC.

The seller must provide you with complete records to identify the puppy. The AKC requires that the seller provide the buyer with the following: breed; sex, color and markings; date of birth; litter number (when available); names and registration numbers of the parents; breeder's name; and date sold or delivered.

teeth and other problems. Veterinary bills may soon distort initial savings into financial or, worse, emotional loss.

Inquire about inoculations and when the puppy was last dosed for worms. Check the ears. Although many puppies do not have erect ears until five or six months, some movement forward and signs of lifting when the puppy is alerted are good predictors of normal development.

YOUR SCHEDULE ...

If you lead an erratic, unpredictable life, with daily or weekly changes in your work requirements, consider the problems of owning a puppy. The new puppy has to be fed regularly, socialized (loved, petted, handled, introduced to other people) and, most importantly, allowed to go outdoors for house-training. As the dog gets older, he can be more tolerant of deviations in his feeding and relief schedule.

Approach the dam and her puppies. The dam should be friendly and trusting. The puppies should be outgoing and interested in meeting you. Do not be concerned if the litter is limited to two or three pups. Yorkies have very small litters, and a single puppy is not uncommon. The breeder may not be able to give you "pick of the litter," since the number of puppies is so limited. Additionally, do not be taken aback if the breeder whom you have selected tells you that there is a six months' to two years' waiting period for a puppy. Since Yorkshires have such small litters and the demand for the breed is high, breeders commonly cannot meet the demand. This is especially true with breeders who have established reputations. Perhaps your chosen breeder can recommend another breeder who has puppies available sooner. If not, you may have to wait for the puppy of your choice.

COMMITMENT OF OWNERSHIP
After considering all of these factors, you have most likely already made some very important decisions about selecting your puppy. You have chosen the Yorkshire Terrier, which means that you have decided which characteristics you want in a dog and what type of dog will best fit into your family and lifestyle. If

BOY OR GIRL?

An important consideration to be discussed is the sex of your puppy. For a family companion, a bitch may be the better choice, considering the female's inbred concern for all young creatures and her accompanying tolerance and patience. It is always advisable to spay a pet bitch, which may guarantee her a longer life.

A Yorkie dam with five of her puppies. This is an unusually large litter for a Yorkshire Terrier, as litters of one or two are far more common.

you have selected a breeder, you have gone a step further—you have done your research and found a responsible, conscientious person who breeds quality Yorkshire Terriers and who should become a reliable source of help as you and your puppy adjust to life together. If you have observed a litter in action, you have obtained a firsthand look at the dynamics of a puppy "pack" and, thus, you have gotten to learn about each pup's individual personality—perhaps you have even found one that particularly appeals to you.

However, even if you have

Yorkie puppies's ears become erect in time. Breeders explain that the teething period often interferes with the ears, which will re-stand after the phase is over.

Yorkshire Terriers are lovers from the beginning. They quickly bond to their human friends. This warmth is one of the reasons for their huge popularity.

on the way to dog ownership. It may seem like a lot of effort…and you have not even brought the pup home yet! Remember, though, you cannot be too careful when it comes to deciding on the type of dog you want and finding out about your prospective pup's background. Buying a puppy is not—or *should* not be—just another whimsical purchase. In fact, this is one instance in which you actually *do* get to choose your

not yet found the Yorkshire Terrier puppy of your dreams, observing pups will help you learn to recognize certain behavior and to determine what a pup's behavior indicates about his temperament. You will be able to pick out which pups are the leaders, which ones are less outgoing, which ones are confident, which ones are shy, playful, etc. Equally as important, you will learn to recognize what a healthy pup should look and act like. All of these things will help you in your search, and when you find the Yorkshire Terrier that was meant for you, you will know it!

Researching your breed, selecting a responsible breeder and observing as many pups as possible are all important steps

ARE YOU PREPARED?

Unfortunately, when a puppy is bought by someone who does not take into consideration the time and attention that dog ownership requires, it is the puppy who suffers when he is either abandoned or placed in a shelter by a frustrated owner. So all of the "homework" you do in preparation for your pup's arrival will benefit you both. The more informed you are, the more you will know what to expect and the better equipped you will be to handle the ups and downs of raising a puppy. Hopefully, everyone in the household is willing to do his part in raising and caring for the pup. The anticipation of owning a dog often brings a lot of promises from excited family members: "I will walk him every day," "I will feed him," "I will house-train him," etc., but these things take time and effort, and promises can easily be forgotten once the novelty of the new pet has worn off.

PET INSURANCE

Just like you can insure your car, your house and your own health, you likewise can insure your dog's health. Investigate a pet insurance policy by talking to your vet. Depending on the age of your dog, the breed and the kind of coverage you desire, your policy can be very affordable. Most policies cover accidental injuries, poisoning and thousands of medical problems and illnesses, including cancers. Some carriers also offer routine care and immunization coverage, though these are more costly.

Always keep in mind that a puppy is nothing more than a baby in a furry disguise...a baby who is virtually helpless in a human world and who trusts his owner for fulfillment of his basic needs for survival. That goes beyond food, water and shelter; your pup needs care, protection, guidance and love. If you are not prepared to commit to this, then you are not prepared to own a dog.

"Wait a minute," you say. "How hard could this be? All of my neighbors own dogs and they seem to be doing just fine. Why should I have to worry about all of this?" Well, you should not worry about it; in fact, you will

Observe as many Yorkie pups as possible so you can judge normal puppy behavior, how a healthy puppy reacts to you and other stimuli and how the pup feels when you handle him.

own family! But, you may be thinking, buying a puppy should be fun—it should not be so serious and involved. If you keep in mind the thought that your puppy is not a cuddly stuffed toy or glass ornament, but instead will become a real member of your family, you will realize that, while buying a puppy is a pleasurable and exciting endeavor, it is not something to be taken lightly. Relax...the fun will start when the pup comes home!

A veterinarian should have examined the parents of your puppy before they were bred to ascertain whether any inherited eye (or other) abnormalities could be passed to their puppies.

PREPARING PUPPY'S PLACE IN YOUR HOME

Researching your breed and finding a breeder are only two aspects of the "homework" you will have to do before bringing your Yorkshire Terrier puppy home. You will also have to prepare your home and family for the new addition. Much like you would prepare a nursery for a newborn baby, you will need to designate a place in your home that will be the puppy's own. How you prepare your home will depend on how much freedom the dog will be allowed: will he be confined to one room or a specific area in the house, or will he be allowed to roam as he

probably find that once your Yorkshire Terrier pup gets used to his new home, he will fall into his place in the family quite naturally. But it never hurts to emphasize the commitment of dog ownership. With some time and patience, it is really not too difficult to raise a curious and exuberant Yorkshire Terrier pup to become a well-adjusted and well-mannered adult dog—a dog that could become your most loyal friend.

TEMPERAMENT COUNTS

Your selection of a good puppy can be determined by your needs. A show potential or a good pet? It is your choice. Every puppy, however, should be of good temperament. Although show-quality puppies are bred and raised with emphasis on physical conformation, responsible breeders strive for equally good temperament. Do not buy from a breeder who concentrates solely on physical beauty at the expense of personality.

pleases? Whatever you decide, you must ensure that he has a place that he can "call his own."

When you bring your new puppy into your home, you are bringing him into what will become his home as well. Obviously, you did not buy a puppy so that he could rule the roost, but in order for a puppy to grow into a stable, well-adjusted dog, he has to feel comfortable in his surroundings. Remember, he is leaving the warmth and security of his mother and littermates, plus the familiarity of the only place he has ever known, so it is important to make his transition as easy as possible. By preparing a place in your home for the puppy, you are making him feel as welcome as possible in a strange new place. It should not take him long to get used to it, but the sudden shock of being transplanted is somewhat traumatic for a young pup. Imagine how a small child would feel in the same situation—that is how your puppy must be feeling. It is up to you to reassure him and to let him know, "Little fellow, you are going to like it here!"

WHAT YOU SHOULD BUY

CRATE

To someone unfamiliar with the use of crates in dog training, it may seem like punishment to shut a dog in a crate; this is not

TIME TO GO HOME
Breeders rarely release Yorkie puppies until they are 12 weeks of age, which is later than for most larger breeds who are released around 8 weeks. If a breeder has a puppy that is older than 12 weeks of age, he is likely well socialized and house-trained. Be sure that he is otherwise healthy before deciding to take him home.

the case at all. Crates are not cruel—crates have many humane and highly effective uses in dog care and training. For example, crate training is a very popular and very successful housebreaking method; a crate can keep your dog safe during travel; and, perhaps most importantly, a crate provides your dog with a place of

Your Yorkie puppy will enjoy the grass, especially when it is comfortably warm, but keep in mind that fleas, ticks and other parasitic organisms can lurk in the grass.

Breeders train their puppies never to defecate or eliminate in their clean sleeping areas. Crate training continues this philosophy and requires the owner to use a crate once the Yorkie pup arrives home.

his own in your home. It serves as a "doggie bedroom" of sorts—your Yorkshire Terrier can curl up in his crate when he wants to sleep or when he just needs a break. Many dogs sleep in their crates overnight. With a nice plush crate pad and a favorite toy, a crate becomes a cozy pseudo-den for your dog. Like his ancestors, he too will seek out the comfort and retreat of a den—you just happen to be providing him with something a little more luxurious than leaves and twigs lining a dirty ditch.

As far as purchasing a crate, the type that you buy is up to you.

It will most likely be one of the two most popular types: wire or fiberglass. There are advantages and disadvantages to each type. For example, a wire crate is more open, allowing the air to flow through and affording the dog a view of what is going on around him. A fiberglass crate, however, is sturdier and can double as a travel crate since it provides more protection for the dog. Purchase the smallest crate available from the pet shop. This crate will suit the Yorkie in puppyhood and adulthood—a real advantage to choosing one of the smallest breeds known to man!

BEDDING

A crate pad in the dog's crate will help the dog feel more at home. You can add a blanket in the cooler months. First, the bedding will take the place of the leaves, twigs, etc., that the pup would use in the wild to make a den; the pup can make his own "burrow" in the crate. Although your pup is far removed from his den-making ancestors, the denning instinct is still a part of his genetic makeup. Second, until you bring your pup home, he has been sleeping amid the warmth of his mother and litter-mates, and while a blanket is not the same as a warm, breathing body, it still provides heat and something with which to snuggle. You will want to wash your

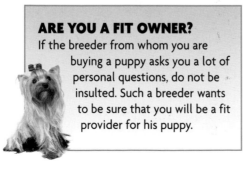

ARE YOU A FIT OWNER?
If the breeder from whom you are buying a puppy asks you a lot of personal questions, do not be insulted. Such a breeder wants to be sure that you will be a fit provider for his puppy.

your expensive shoes and leather sofa. Puppies love to chew; in fact, chewing is a physical need for pups as they are teething, and everything looks appetizing! The full range of your possessions—from cotton slipper to Oriental rug—is fair game in the eyes of a teething pup. Puppies are not all that discerning when it comes to finding something to literally "sink their teeth into"—everything tastes great!

CRATE TIP

If you must keep your Yorkie crated during the day while you are at work, be sure to make extra effort when you are at home to spend time with him and include him in your activities.

pup's bedding frequently in case he has an accident in his crate, and replace or remove any blanket or padding that becomes ragged and starts to fall apart.

Toys

Toys are a must for dogs of all ages, especially for curious playful pups. Puppies are the "children" of the dog world, and what child does not love toys? Chew toys provide enjoyment to both dog and owner—your dog will enjoy playing with his favorite toys, while you will enjoy the fact that they distract him from

Your local pet shop will have many crates of different sizes and styles. A small-sized crate will accommodate your Yorkie in puppyhood and adulthood.

PHOTO COURTESY OF MIKKI PET PRODUCTS.

Provide your Yorkie with safe chew toys that are made specifically for dogs. Whenever the dog wants to chew on something inappropriate, give him his bone instead.

Provide your Yorkie with durable chew toys made for smaller dogs. Stuffed toys are another option; these are good to put in the dog's crate to give him some company. Be careful of these, as a pup can de-stuff one pretty quickly, and stay away from stuffed toys with small plastic eyes or parts that a pup could choke on. Similarly, squeaky toys are quite popular. There are dogs that will come running from anywhere in the house at the first sound from their favorite squeaky friend. Again, if a pup de-stuffs one of these, the small plastic squeaker inside can be dangerous if swallowed. Monitor the condition of all of your pup's toys carefully and get rid of any that have been chewed to the point of becoming potentially dangerous.

Be careful of natural bones, which have a tendency to splinter into sharp, dangerous pieces. Also be careful of rawhide, which after enough chewing can turn into pieces that are easy to swallow, and also watch out for the mushy mess it can turn into on your carpet.

LEASH
A nylon leash is probably the best option, as it is the most

TOYS, TOYS, TOYS!
With a big variety of dog toys available, and so many that look like they would be a lot of fun for a dog, be careful in your selection. It is amazing what a set of puppy teeth can do to an innocent-looking toy; so, obviously, safety is a major consideration. Be sure to choose the most durable products that you can find. Hard nylon bones and toys are a safe bet, and many of them are offered in different scents and flavors that will be sure to capture your Yorshire Terrier's attention. It is always fun to play a game of fetch with your dog, and there are balls and flying discs that are specially made to withstand dog teeth.

Your local pet shop will have a large assortment of toys suitable for your Yorkie.

resistant to puppy teeth should your pup take a liking to chewing on his leash. Of course, this is a habit that should be nipped in the bud, but if your pup likes to chew on his leash he has a very

MENTAL AND DENTAL

Toys not only help your puppy get the physical and mental stimulation he needs but also provide a great way to keep his teeth clean. Hard rubber or nylon toys, especially those constructed with grooves, are designed to scrape away plaque, preventing bad breath and gum infection.

slim chance of being able to chew through the strong nylon. Nylon leashes are also light-weight, which is good for a young Yorkshire Terrier who is just getting used to the idea of walking on a leash. For everyday walking and safety purposes, the nylon leash is a good choice. As your pup grows up and gets used to walking on the leash, and can do it politely, you may want to purchase a flexible leash, which allows you either to extend the length to give the dog a broader area to explore or to pull in the leash when you want to keep him close.

Your local pet shop will have a large variety of leashes in different colors and made from different materials.

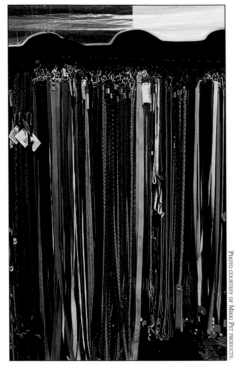

PHOTO COURTESY OF MIKKI PET PRODUCTS.

COLLAR

Your pup should get used to wearing a collar all the time since you will want to attach his ID tags to his collar. Also, the leash and collar go hand in hand—you have to attach the leash to something! A lightweight nylon collar will be a good choice; make sure that it fits snugly enough so that the pup cannot wriggle out of it, but is loose enough so that it will not be uncomfortably tight around the pup's neck. You should be able to fit a finger in between the pup and the collar. It may take some time for your pup to get used to wearing the collar, but soon he will not even notice that it is there.

FOOD AND WATER BOWLS

Your pup will need two bowls, one for food and one for water. You may want two sets of bowls, one for inside and one for outside, depending on where the dog will be fed, although Yorkies typically spend most of their time indoors. Stainless steel or sturdy plastic bowls are popular choices. Although plastic bowls are more chewable, dogs tend not to chew on the steel variety, which can also be sterilized.

CLEANING SUPPLIES

Until a pup is house-trained, you will be doing a lot of cleaning. Accidents will occur, which is okay for now because he does not know any better. All you can do is clean up any accidents—old rags, paper towels, newspapers, bath towels and a safe disinfectant are good to have on hand. Be sure that you thoroughly remove the odor from any mishaps. Dogs tend to repeat offenses when they can detect a familiar scent.

BEYOND THE BASICS

The items previously discussed are the bare necessities. You will find out what else you need as you go along—grooming supplies, bows, flea/tick protection, baby gates to partition a room, etc.—these things will vary depending on your situation. It is just important that right away you have everything you need to feed and make your Yorkshire Terrier comfortable in his first few days at home.

PUPPY-PROOFING YOUR HOME
Aside from making sure that your Yorkshire Terrier will be comfortable in your home, you also have to make sure that your home is safe for your Yorkshire Terrier. This means taking precautions to make sure that your pup will not get into anything he should not

As your Yorkie gets older, his need for frequent feedings will diminish. Adult Yorkies usually require one or two meals per day.

get into and that there is nothing within his reach that may harm him should he sniff it, chew it, inspect it, etc. This probably seems obvious since, while you are primarily concerned with your pup's safety, at the same time you do not want your belongings to be ruined. Breakables should be placed out of reach if your dog is to have full run of the house. If he is to be limited to certain places within the house, keep any potentially dangerous items in the "off-limits" areas. An electrical cord can pose a danger should the puppy decide to taste it—and who is going to convince a pup that it would not make a great chew toy? Cords should be fastened tightly against the wall, out of the Yorkie's sight. If your dog is going to spend time in a crate, make sure that there is nothing near his crate that he can reach if he sticks his curious little nose or paws through the openings. And just as you would

CRATE-TRAINING TIPS
During crate training, you should partition off the section of the crate in which the pup stays. If he is given too big an area, this will hinder your training efforts. Crate training is based on the fact that a dog does not like to soil his sleeping quarters, so it is ineffective to keep a pup in an area that is so big that he can eliminate in one end and get far enough away from it to sleep. Also, you want to make the crate den-like for the pup. Blankets and a favorite toy will make the crate cozy for the small pup; as he grows, you may want to evict some of his "roommates" to make more room. It will take some coaxing at first, but be patient. Given some time to get used to it, your pup will adapt to his new home-within-a-home quite nicely.

Flowers attract Yorkies because of their colors and scents. Remember that flowers also attract insects that bite dogs, so be careful.

with a child, keep all household cleaners and chemicals where the pup cannot get to them.

It is just as important to make sure that the outside of your home is safe. Of course, your puppy should never be unsupervised, but a pup let loose in the yard will want to run and explore, and he should be granted that freedom. Do not let a fence give you a false sense of security; you would be surprised how crafty (and persistent) a dog can be in figuring out how to dig under and squeeze his way through small holes, or to climb

over a fence. It doesn't require a very large gap for a Yorkie to escape, and don't forget that the Yorkie is an earth dog and is gifted at digging. Be sure to repair or secure any gaps in the fence. Check the fence periodically to ensure that it is in good shape and make repairs as needed; a very determined pup may return to the same spot to "work on it" until he is able to get through.

FIRST TRIP TO THE VET
Okay, you have picked out your puppy, your home and family are ready, now all you have to do is pick your Yorkshire Terrier up from the breeder and the fun begins, right? Well...not so fast. Something else you need to prepare for is your pup's first trip to the veterinarian. Perhaps the breeder can recommend someone in the area who specializes in Yorkshire Terriers or toy dogs, or maybe you know some other Yorkshire Terrier owners who can suggest a good vet. Either way, you should have an appointment arranged for your pup before you pick him up; plan on taking him for a checkup within the first few days of bringing him home.

The pup's first visit will consist of an overall examination to make sure that the pup does not have any problems that are not apparent to you. The veteri-

THE RIDE HOME

Taking your dog from the breeder to your home in a car can be a very uncomfortable experience for both of you. The puppy will have been taken from his warm, friendly, safe environment and brought into a strange new environment—an environment that moves! Be prepared for loose bowels, urination, crying, whining and even fear biting. With proper love and encouragement when you arrive home, the stress of the trip should quickly disappear.

Your vet should give your new Yorkie a thorough examination. Be conscientious and make note of any advice that the vet gives you regarding the future care of your pet.

narian will also set up a schedule for the pup's vaccinations; the breeder will inform you of which ones the pup has already received and the vet can continue from there.

INTRODUCTION TO THE FAMILY

Everyone in the house will be excited about the puppy's coming home and will want to pet him and play with him, but it is best to make the introduction low-key so as not to overwhelm the puppy. He is apprehensive already; it is the first time he has been separated from his mother and the breeder, and the ride to your home is likely the first time he has been in a car. The last thing you want to do is smother him, as this will only frighten him further. This is not to say that human contact is not extremely necessary at this stage, because this is the time when an instant connection between the pup and his human family are formed. Gentle petting and soothing words should help console him, as well as just putting him down and letting him explore on his own (under your watchful eye, of course).

Yorkie babies are adorable and affectionate. Meeting a litter is quite an experience, and you'll likely find it difficult to choose just one!

The pup may approach the family members or may busy himself with exploring for a while. Gradually, each person should spend some time with the pup, one at a time, crouching down to get as close to the pup's level as possible, letting him sniff their hands and petting him gently. He definitely needs human attention and he needs to be touched—this is how to form an immediate bond. Just remember that the pup is experiencing a lot of things for the first time, all at the same time. There are new people, new noises, new smells and new things to investigate, so be gentle and be affectionate.

Don't overwhelm your new Yorkshire Terrier during his first days in your home. He has his whole life to explore and experience the world around him.

PUP'S FIRST NIGHT HOME

You have traveled home with your new charge safely in his crate. He's been to the vet for a thorough checkup; he has been weighed, his papers examined; perhaps he has even been vaccinated and wormed as well. He has met the family and licked the whole family, including the excited children and the less-than-happy cat. He has explored his area, his new bed, the yard and anywhere else he has been permitted. He has eaten his first meal at home and relieved himself in the proper place. He has heard lots of new sounds, smelled new friends and seen more of the outside world than ever before.

That was the just the first day! He is worn out and is ready for bed...or so you think!

It is puppy's first night and you are ready to say "Good night"—keep in mind that this is puppy's first night ever to be sleeping alone. His dam and littermates are no longer at paw's length and he is a bit scared, cold and lonely. Be reassuring to your new family member, but this is not the time to spoil him and give in to his inevitable whining.

IN DUE TIME
It will take at least two weeks for your puppy to become accustomed to his new surroundings. Give him lots of love, attention, handling, frequent opportunities to relieve himself, a diet he likes to eat and a place he can call his own.

Puppies whine. They whine to let others know where they are and hopefully to get company out of it. Place your pup in his bed or crate in his room and close the crate door. Mercifully, he will fall asleep without a peep. When the inevitable occurs, ignore the whining. Be strong and keep his interest in mind. Do not allow your heart to become guilty and visit the pup. He will fall asleep.

Many breeders recommend placing a piece of bedding from his former homestead in his new bed so that he recognizes the scent of his littermates. Others still advise placing a hot water bottle in his bed for warmth. This latter may be a good idea provided the pup does not attempt to suckle—he will get good and wet and may not fall asleep so fast.

Puppy's first night can be somewhat stressful for the pup and his new family. Remember that you are setting the tone of nighttime at your house. Unless you want to play with your pup every night at 10 p.m., midnight and 2 a.m., do not initiate the habit. Surely your family will thank you, and so will your pup!

PREVENTING PUPPY PROBLEMS

SOCIALIZATION
Now that you have done all of the preparatory work and have helped your pup get accustomed to his new home and family, it is about time for you to have some fun! Socializing your Yorkshire Terrier pup gives you the opportunity to show off your new

Don't play too roughly with your Yorkie. Keep in mind that, despite your Yorkie's big-dog confidence, he's still a petite fellow that must be handled with care.

friend, and your pup gets to reap the benefits of being an adorable furry creature that people will fuss over, want to pet and, in general, think is absolutely precious!

Besides getting to know his new family, your puppy should be exposed to other people, animals and situations. This will help him become well adjusted as he grows up and less prone to being timid or fearful of the new things he will encounter. Your pup's socialization began at the breeder's; now it is your responsibility to continue. This early socialization is most critical, as

DOG MEETS WORLD
Thorough socialization includes not only meeting new people but also being introduced to new experiences such as riding in the car, having his coat brushed, hearing the television, walking in a crowd—the list is endless. The more your Yorkie experiences, and the more positive the experiences are, the less of a shock and the less frightening it will be for your dog to encounter new things.

Having a parrot sit on your Yorkie puppy's head would qualify as a "new experience" for your dog. Keep socialization in perspective—don't overwhelm your pup with too much activity.

this is the time when he forms his impressions of the outside world. Lack of socialization can manifest itself in fear and aggression as the dog grows up. He needs lots of human contact, affection, handling and exposure to other animals. Your Yorkie puppy will still be with the breeder during the eight-to-ten-week-old period, also known as the fear period. The interaction he receives during this time should be gentle and reassuring.

Once your pup has received his necessary vaccinations, feel free to take him out and about (on his leash, of course). Take him around the neighborhood, take him on your daily errands, let people pet him, let him meet other dogs and pets, etc. Puppies do not have to try to make friends; there will be no shortage of people who will want to introduce themselves. Just make sure that you carefully supervise each meeting. If the neighborhood children want to say hello, for example, that is great—children and pups most often make great companions. But sometimes an excited child can unintentionally handle a pup too roughly, or an overzealous pup can playfully nip a little too hard. You want to make socialization experiences positive ones; what a pup learns during this very formative stage will impact his attitude toward future encounters. A pup that has a bad experience with a child may grow up to be a dog that is shy around or aggressive toward children, and you want your dog to be comfortable around everyone he meets.

CONSISTENCY IN TRAINING

Dogs, being pack animals, naturally need a leader, or else they try to establish dominance in their packs. When you bring a dog into your family, who becomes the leader and who

CHEWING TIPS

Chewing goes hand in hand with nipping in the sense that a teething puppy is always looking for a way to soothe his aching gums. In this case, instead of chewing on you, he may have taken a liking to your favorite shoe or something else which he should not be chewing. Again, realize that this is a normal canine behavior that does not need to be discouraged, only redirected. Your pup just needs to be taught what is acceptable to chew on and what is off-limits. Consistently tell him "No!" when you catch him chewing on something forbidden and give him a chew toy.

Conversely, praise him when you catch him chewing on something appropriate. In this way, you are discouraging the inappropriate behavior and reinforcing the desired behavior. The puppy's chewing should stop after his adult teeth have come in, but an adult dog continues to chew for various reasons—perhaps because he is bored, needs to relieve tension or just likes to chew. That is why it is important to redirect his chewing when he is still young.

becomes the "pack" is entirely up to you! Your pup's intuitive quest for dominance, coupled with the fact that it is nearly impossible to look at an adorable Yorkshire Terrier pup, with his "puppy-dog" eyes, and not cave in, give the pup almost an unfair advantage in getting the upper hand!

And a pup will definitely test the waters to see what he can and cannot get away with. Do not give in to those pleading eyes—stand your ground when it comes to disciplining the pup and make sure that all family members do the same. It will only confuse the pup when Mother tells him to get off the couch when he is used to sitting up there with Father to watch the nightly news. Avoid discrepancies by having all members of the household decide on the rules before the pup even comes home...and be consistent in enforcing them! Early training shapes the dog's personality.

COMMON PUPPY PROBLEMS
The best way to prevent problems is to be proactive in stop-

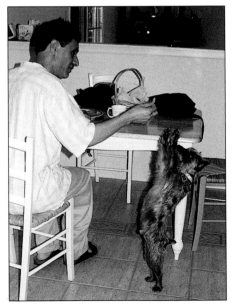

Even if your Yorkie cries, whines and begs, don't feed him from the table or you will have a beggar for life. Besides, human food can spoil your Yorkie's balanced diet.

> **PROPER SOCIALIZATION**
> The socialization period for puppies is from age 8 to 16 weeks. This is the time when puppies need to leave their birth family and take up residence with their new owners, where they will meet many new people, other pets, etc. Failure to be adequately socialized can cause the dog to grow up fearing others and being shy and unfriendly.

ping an undesirable behavior as soon as it starts. The old saying "You can't teach an old dog new tricks" does not necessarily hold true, but it is true that it *is* much easier to discourage bad behavior in a young developing pup than to wait until the pup's bad behavior becomes the adult dog's bad habit. There are some problems that are especially prevalent in puppies as they develop.

NIPPING
As puppies start to teethe, they feel the need to sink their teeth into anything...unfortunately, that includes your fingers, arms, hair, toes...whatever happens to be available. You may find this behavior cute for about the first five seconds...until you feel just how sharp those puppy teeth are. This is something you want to discourage immediately and consistently with a firm "No!" (or whatever number of firm "Nos" it takes for him to understand that you mean business) and replace

your finger with an appropriate chew toy. While this behavior is merely annoying when the dog is still young, it can become dangerous as your Yorkshire Terrier's adult teeth grow in and his jaws develop, if he thinks that it is okay to gnaw on human appendages.

CRYING/WHINING

Your pup will often cry, whine, whimper, howl or make some type of commotion when he is left alone. This is basically his way of calling out for attention, of calling out to make sure that you know he is there and that you have not forgotten about him. He feels insecure when he is left alone, for example, when you are out of the house and he is in his crate or when you are in another part of the house and he cannot see you. The noise he is making is an expression of the anxiety he feels at being alone, so he needs to be taught that being alone is okay. You are not actually training the dog to stop making noise, you are training him to feel comfortable when he is alone and thus removing the need for him to make the noise. This is where the crate comes in handy. You want to know that he is safe when you are not there to supervise, and you know that he will be safe in his crate rather than roaming freely about the house. In order for the pup to stay in his crate without making a fuss, he needs to be comfortable in his crate. On that note, it is extremely important that the crate is never used as a form of punishment, or the pup will develop a negative association with the crate.

Accustom the pup to the crate in short, gradually increasing time intervals in which you put him in the crate, maybe with a treat, and stay in the room with him. If he cries or makes a fuss, do not go to him, but stay in his sight. Gradually he will realize that staying in his crate is all right without your help, and it will not be so traumatic for him when you are not around. You may want to leave the radio on softly when you leave the house; the sound of human voices may be comforting to him.

PUPPY PROBLEMS

The majority of problems that are commonly seen in young pups will disappear as your dog gets older. However, how you deal with problems when he is young will determine how he reacts to discipline as an adult dog. It is important to establish who is boss (hopefully it will be you!) right away when you are first bonding with your dog. This bond will set the tone for the rest of your life together.

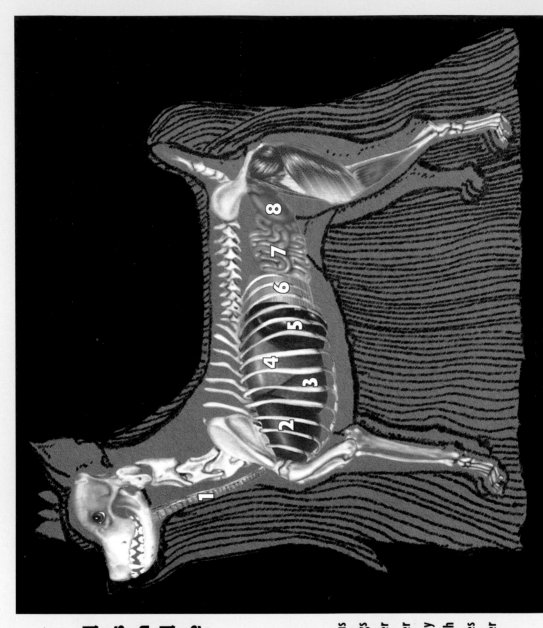

Internal Organs with Skeletal Structure

1. Esophagus
2. Lungs
3. Gall Bladder
4. Liver
5. Kidney
6. Stomach
7. Intestines
8. Urinary Bladder

Everyday Care of Your Yorkshire Terrier

DIETARY AND FEEDING CONSIDERATIONS

You have probably heard it a thousand times—you are what you eat. Believe it or not, it is very true. For dogs, they are what you feed them because they have little choice in the matter. Even those people who truly want to feed their dogs the best often cannot do so because they do not know which foods are best for their dogs.

Dog foods are produced in three basic types: dry, semi-moist and canned. Dry foods are for the cost conscious because they are much less expensive than semi-moist and canned. Dry foods contain the least fat and the most preservatives. Most canned foods are 60–70% water, while semi-moist foods are so full of sugar

The diet for your new Yorkie puppy should be recommended by the breeder and/or your vet. The idea is not to change the puppy's diet too radically or too fast from what was being fed at the breeder's.

that they are the least preferred by owners, though dogs welcome them (as does a child candy).

Three stages of development must be considered when selecting a diet for your dog: the puppy stage, the adult stage and the senior stage.

PUPPY STAGE

Puppies have a natural instinct to suck milk from their mother's breasts. They should exhibit this behavior the first day of their lives. If they do not suckle within a few hours, the breeder attempts to put them onto their mother's

---

TEST FOR PROPER DIET

A good test for proper diet is the color, odor and firmness of your dog's stool. A healthy dog usually produces three semi-hard stools per day. The stools should have no unpleasant odor. They should be the same color from excretion to excretion.

Puppies should be allowed to nurse for at least six weeks. They need their mother's milk for protection against many diseases.

nipples. Their failure to feed means that the breeder has to feed them himself. This will involve a baby bottle and a special formula. Their mother's milk is much better than any formula because it contains colostrum, a sort of antibiotic milk, which protects the puppy during the first eight to ten weeks of their lives.

Puppies should be allowed to nurse for six weeks and they should be slowly weaned away from their mother by introducing small portions of canned meat after they are about one month old. The first three weeks of the Yorkshire Terrier puppy's life require extra caution from the breeder as the breed, due to its small size, is susceptible to neonatal hypoglycemia, also called low blood sugar. Hypoglycemia is a concern of most of the toy breeds, and in very young pups the concern is due to the limited reserves of glyco-

gen and the fact that the dog's liver enzymes are not yet functioning fully. For this reason, supplemental feedings are needed. Hypoglycemia can be expressed in shaking, tremors and nervousness. Discuss the condition with your vet so that you are prepared to treat any incidence in a young pup.

By the time they are eight weeks old, the pups should be completely weaned and fed solely a good puppy food. During the weaning period, their diet is most important as puppies grow fastest during their first year of life. Growth foods can be recommended by your veterinarian, and the puppy should be kept on this diet for 9 to 12 months. Puppy diets should be balanced for your

GRAIN-BASED DIETS
Some less expensive dog foods are based on grains and other plant proteins. While these products may appear to be attractively priced, many breeders prefer a diet based on animal proteins and believe that they are more conducive to your dog's health. Many grain-based diets rely on soy protein, which may cause flatulence (passing gas).

There are many cases, however, when your dog might require a special diet. These special requirements should only be recommended by your veterinarian.

With the delicate beauty of a porcelain doll, the Yorkie is aptly classified as a Toy breed. A dog, however, is *not* a toy.

There is no single best diet for Yorkies—or any other breed, for that matter. With a coat breed like the Yorkshire Terrier, a proper balanced diet shines through in every glistening hair.

dog's needs and supplements of vitamins, minerals and protein should not be necessary.

ADULT DIETS

A dog is considered an adult when he has stopped growing. The growth is in height and/or length. Do not consider the dog's weight when the decision is made to switch from a puppy diet to a maintenance diet. Again you should rely upon your veterinarian to recommend an acceptable maintenance diet. Major dog-food manufacturers specialize in this type of food and it is necessary for you to select the one best suited to your dog's needs. Active dogs have different requirements than sedate dogs. A Yorkshire Terrier reaches adulthood at about two years of age, though some dogs mature as late as three years.

SENIOR DIETS

At around seven or eight years of age, the Yorkshire Terrier can be considered a senior. As dogs get older, their metabolism changes. The older dog usually exercises less, moves more slowly and sleeps more. This change in lifestyle and physiological performance requires a change in diet. Since these changes take place slowly, they might not be recognizable. What is easily recognizable is weight gain. By continuing to feed your dog an adult-maintenance diet when he is slowing down metabolically, your dog will gain weight. Obesity in an older dog compounds the health problems that already accompany old age.

As your dog gets older, few of his organs function up to par. The kidneys slow down and the intestines become less efficient. These age-related factors are best handled with a change in diet and a change in feeding schedule to give smaller portions that are more easily digested.

There is no single best diet for every older dog. While many dogs do well on light or senior diets, other dogs do better on puppy diets or other special premium diets such as lamb and rice. Be sensitive to your senior Yorkshire Terrier's diet and this will help control other problems that may arise with your old friend.

WATER

Just as your dog needs proper nutrition from his food, water is an essential "nutrient" as well. Water keeps the dog's body properly hydrated and promotes normal function of the body's systems. During housebreaking, it is necessary to keep an eye on how much water your Yorkshire Terrier is drinking, but once he is reliably trained he should have access to clean fresh water at all times. Make sure that the dog's water bowl is clean, and change the water often.

EXERCISE

All dogs require some form of exercise, regardless of the breed. A sedentary lifestyle is as harmful

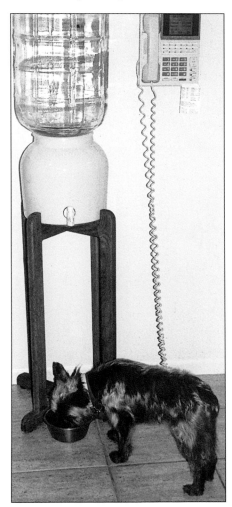

Providing your dog with clean fresh water is a basic requirement of ownership. Some owners prefer to offer only filtered or bottled water to their dogs.

to a dog as it is to a person. Fortunately for the Yorkshire Terrier owner, meeting the breed's requirements is simple. Regular walks, play sessions with you around the neighborhood, or letting the dog run free in the yard under your supervision are all sufficient forms of exercise for the Yorkshire Terrier. Not only is exercise essential to keep the dog's body fit, it is essential to his mental well-being. A bored dog will find something to do, which often manifests itself in some type of destructive behavior. In this sense, it is essential for the owner's mental well-being as well!

Keeping a Yorkshire Terrier in a full-length show coat requires daily commitment of the owner. While having such a glamorous toy dog around the home is rewarding, it's a decision the owner must make.

GROOMING

Whereas the Yorkshire Terrier does not require much special care or accommodation in terms of feeding, exercise or space, the care of the coat does place considerable demands on the owner. Grooming is not the breeder's first concern for the Yorkshire Terrier's coat. Any experienced dog person will agree with the adage, "First you breed a coat, then you feed a coat." Combing, brushing and bathing are secondary. Nevertheless, the Yorkshire Terrier is a true "coat breed," which means his long, silky hair in his unique blue coloration is one of his hallmarks.

Keeping the Yorkie in a full-length coat requires special care and is usually only pursued by the show set. Pet owners usually keep the Yorkie's coat trimmed to a manageable length. Indeed the dog's fall (tuft of hair on the head) can impede the Yorkie's eating (by dangling into the food bowl), and the characteristic mustache and beard can easily be damaged in chewing and playing. A Yorkie kept in full coat must be supervised when exercising or playing since the coat is easily damaged and tangled. Most owners tie the coat up so that the dog can maneuver about more freely and enjoy frolicking about in the yard. Pet owners should never sacrifice exercise and sunshine for the sake of a long coat.

Owners of show Yorkies must

familiarize themselves with the art of wrapping the Yorkie coat, a very complicated procedure involving over two dozen "paper wraps." By wrapping the coat, the coat is protected from breaking off and becoming worn from trailing along the floor. If you are considering keeping the coat at its full length for showing the dog, discuss wrapping with the breeder or another Yorkie expert. It cannot be sufficiently explained in a book and needs to be demonstrated to understand properly.

Accustom the young Yorkie to a daily brushing regimen immediately. There is nothing amusing about wrestling with a Yorkie every morning simply to brush his coat. Most Yorkies welcome the attention, but early acclimation is well advised. For the young puppy, a long bristle brush will help to keep the growing coat neat. Avoid brushing the puppy's face with the brush since a slight slip of the hand can badly injure a Yorkie's eyes. Since puppies tend to be busy, an occasional bath may be in order to keep the baby smelling clean and fresh. If the puppy is still eating wet food, the owner will need to wash the dog's face after every meal. Many owners start the Yorkie on dry food simply to keep the dog as clean as possible.

Daily brushing is effective for removing dead hair and stimulating the dog's natural oils to add

Wash the Yorkie with warm water. Use a very low-pressure spray.

Be careful never to spray directly into your Yorkie's face. Given the delicate nature of the breed's eyes, not to mention keeping the ears dry, spraying the head should be avoided.

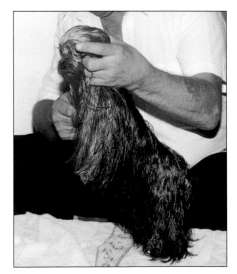

Combing through the Yorkie's hair after a bath should be done gently so as not to damage the coat.

Gentle drying with a blow dryer is preferable to just letting the dog air-dry. The stream of air should be warm, but not hot, so as not to burn the dog's skin.

Use a pin brush to assist in the drying process to avoid creating any knots or tangles in the coat.

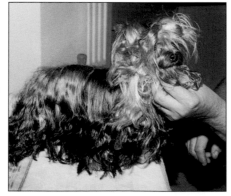

What price glamour! For a dog as naturally beautiful as the Yorkshire Terrier, doesn't this seem like a lot of effort? It's worth it... we're almost finished.

shine and a healthy look to the coat. For the Yorkie, daily brushing will minimize tangles and mats, get rid of dust and dandruff, and remove any dead hair. On the adult, a natural bristle brush used from the skin to the end of the hair, through each layer of hair, is the best course of action. Never skip a day's grooming session or the next day will be more difficult. Over-brushing should be avoided since it inevitably causes split ends. The application of oil or lanolin is recommended by most breeders in order to keep the Yorkshire's lustrous coat looking its best. Oil stimulates the hair and prevents the hair from becoming matted.

BATHING

Dogs do not need to be bathed as often as humans, but bathing as needed is essential for healthy skin and a healthy, shiny coat. Again, like most anything, if you accustom your pup to being bathed as a puppy, it will be second nature by the time he grows up. You want your dog to be at ease in the bath or else it could end up a wet, soapy, messy ordeal for both of you!

Brush your Yorkshire Terrier thoroughly before wetting his coat. This will get rid of most mats and tangles, which are harder to remove when the coat is wet. Make sure that your dog has a good non-slip surface to stand on. Begin by wetting the dog's coat. A shower or hose attachment is necessary for thoroughly wetting and rinsing the coat. Check the water temperature to make sure that it is neither too hot nor too cold.

Next, apply shampoo to the dog's coat and work it into a good lather. You should purchase a shampoo that is made for dogs; do not use a product made for human hair. Wash the head last; you do not want shampoo to drip into the dog's eyes while you are washing the rest of his body. Work the shampoo all the way down to the skin. You can use this opportunity to check the skin for any bumps, bites or other abnormalities. Do not neglect any area of the body—get all of the hard-to-reach places.

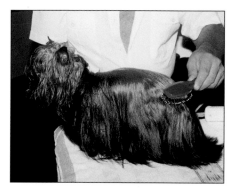

Brushing the damp Yorkie requires a special brush with the ends of the bristles covered with plastic.

Don't forget the top of the head. The topknot is essential to the proper Yorkshire Terrier expression.

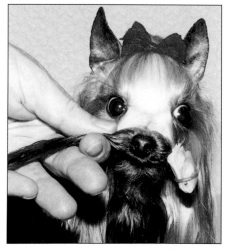

The mustache must be rolled and securely protected with a paper wrapper.

SOAP IT UP

The use of human soap products like shampoo, bubble bath and hand soap can be damaging to a dog's coat and skin. Human products are too strong; they remove the protective oils coating the dog's hair and skin that make him water-resistant. Use only shampoo made especially for dogs. You may like to use a medicated shampoo, which will help to keep external parasites at bay.

Wrapping the Yorkie coat in paper requires an experienced groomer or handler. Don't expect to read this book and then attempt to groom your new show contender. Seek professional assistance if you are interested in showing your Yorkie.

Once the dog has been thoroughly shampooed, he requires an equally thorough rinsing. Shampoo left in the coat can be irritating to the skin. Protect his eyes from the shampoo by shielding them with your hand and directing the flow of water in the opposite direction. You should also avoid getting water in the ear

canal. Be prepared for your dog to shake out his coat—you might want to stand back, but make sure you have a hold on the dog to keep him from running through the house.

EAR CLEANING
The ears should be kept clean and any excess hair inside the ear should be trimmed. Ears can be cleaned with a cotton ball and liquid cleaner or ear powder made especially for dogs. Be on the lookout for any signs of infection or ear-mite infestation. If your Yorkshire Terrier has been shaking his head or scratching at his ears frequently, this usually indicates a problem. If his ears have an unusual odor, this is a sure sign of mite infestation or infection, and a signal to have his ears checked by the veterinarian.

Considering the complexity of this grooming routine, would you like to be the "guinea pig" of an inexperienced beautician?

BOWING THE TOPKNOT
The Yorkshire Terrier, like other long-coated toy breeds, typically sports a topknot on his head. The fall, or the long hair on the head, is gathered and tied with a silky ribbon or bow, contributing to the Yorkshire Terrier's unique expression. When forming a topknot, gather all of the hair from the outside corners of the eyes and the top of the head between the ears and down the neck; brush up together and band or tie it securely. Some breeders prefer to use two bows.

REMOVING TANGLES

Most of the mats and tangles that you will find on your Yorkshire Terrier will be on the underside or belly. Pet shops sell various conditioners and detangler solutions that can help remove tangles. You can shred part of the mat with your fingers and work it out with a comb. Be patient. If you spend the necessary time brushing every day, you should never have to resort to cutting a mat from your dog's coat.

NAIL CLIPPING

Your Yorkshire Terrier should be accustomed to having his nails trimmed at an early age, since it will be part of your maintenance routine throughout his life. Not only does it look nicer, but a dog with long nails can cause injury if he jumps up or if he scratches someone unintentionally. Also, a long nail has a better chance of ripping and bleeding, or of causing the feet to spread. A good rule of thumb is that if you can hear your dog's nails' clicking on the floor when he walks, his nails are too long.

Before you start cutting, make sure you can identify the "quick" in each nail. The quick is a blood vessel that runs through the center of each nail and grows rather close to the end. It will bleed if accidentally cut, which will be quite painful for the dog as it contains nerve endings. Keep

Wrapping the coat of a show dog has two primary purposes: to prevent the hairs' being damaged by dragging on the floor and to insure the longest possible growth of the hair.

some type of clotting agent on hand, such as a styptic pencil or styptic powder (the type used for shaving). This will stop the bleeding quickly when applied to the end of the cut nail. Do not panic if this happens, just stop the bleed-

Every part of the dog must be groomed. Tail hairs are often braided.

To aid in having the Yorkie remain standing during grooming, a can or tin is used to keep him standing up properly.

ing and talk soothingly to your dog. Once he has calmed down, move on to the next nail. It is better to clip a little at a time, particularly with black-nailed dogs.

Hold your pup steady as you begin trimming his nails; you do not want him to make any sudden movements or run away. Talk to him soothingly and stroke his hair as you clip. Holding his foot in your hand, simply take off the end

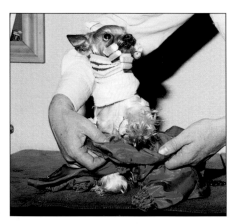

"Are we finished yet?" Can't you just read that in his eyes? The patience of a show Yorkie is legendary.

I'm ready to play now! Such is the life of the show Yorkie. A protective doggy coat can be purchased at quality pet shops or trade stands at dog shows.

Nail Maintenance

Nail Casing

Quick

Cut Line

Dark-Colored Nails

With black or dark nails, it's best to clip only the tip of the nail or to use a file.

Light-Colored Nails

In light-colored nails, clipping is much simpler because you can see the vein (or quick) that grows inside the casing.

of each nail in one quick clip. You can purchase nail clippers that are specially made for dogs; you can probably find them wherever you buy grooming supplies.

TRAVELING WITH YOUR DOG

CAR TRAVEL

You should accustom your Yorkshire Terrier to riding in a car at an early age. You may or may not

The hairs on the bottom of the feet need clipping.

often take him in the car, but at the very least he will need to go to the vet and you do not want these trips to be traumatic for the dog or a big hassle for you. The safest way for a dog to ride in the car is in his crate. If he uses a fiberglass crate in the house, you can use the same crate for travel. If you have a wire crate in the house, consider purchasing an appropriately sized fiberglass or wooden crate for traveling. Wire crates can be used for travel, but fiberglass or wooden crates are safer.

Put the pup in the crate and see how he reacts. If he seems uneasy, you can have a passenger hold him on his lap while you drive. This can be an option for an adult Yorkie, too, provided that the person has a secure hold on the dog. Do not let the dog roam loose in the vehicle—this is very dangerous! If you should stop short, your dog can be thrown and injured. If the dog starts climbing

---

PEDICURE TIP

A dog that spends a lot of time outside on a hard surface, such as cement or pavement, will have his nails naturally worn down and may not need to have them trimmed as often, except maybe in the colder months when he is not outside as much. Regardless, it is best to get your dog accustomed to the nail-trimming procedure at an early age so that he is used to it. Some dogs are especially sensitive about having their feet touched, but if a dog has experienced it since puppyhood, it should not bother him.

As fun as it may seem, a Yorkie traveling uncrated is dangerous for both the dog and driver. Keep him safe and sound in his crate.

on you and pestering you while you are driving, you will not be able to concentrate on the road. It is an unsafe situation for everyone—human and canine.

For long trips, be prepared to stop to let the dog relieve himself. Bring along whatever you need to clean up after him. You should bring along some paper towels and old rags, should he have a potty accident in the car or become carsick.

YORKIES IN THE FRIENDLY SKIES

Contact your chosen airline before proceeding with your travel plans that include your Yorkshire Terrier. The dog will be required to travel in a fiberglass crate and you should always check in advance with the airline regarding specific requirements for the crate's size, type and labeling. To help put the dog at ease, give him one of his favorite toys in the crate. Do not feed the dog for several hours prior to checking in so that you minimize his need to relieve himself. However, some airlines require that the dog must be fed within a certain time frame of arriving at the airport. In any case, a light meal is best.

Make sure your dog is properly identified and that your contact information appears on his ID tags and on his crate. Although most dogs travel in a different area of the plane than the human passengers, the Yorkie is fortunate enough to travel in "coach" (or "first-class") along with his owners! Most airlines provide for toy dogs to travel with their owners, and Yorkie owners should always seek out airlines willing to accommodate their dogs first!

VACATIONS AND BOARDING

So you want to take a family vacation—and you want to include *all* members of the family. You would probably make arrangements for

---

TOO HOT TO HANDLE

Never leave your dog alone in the car. In hot weather, your dog can die from the high temperature inside a closed vehicle; even a car parked in the shade can heat up very quickly. Leaving the window open is dangerous as well since the dog can hurt himself trying to get out.

COLLAR REQUIRED

If your dog gets lost, he is not able to ask for directions home. Identification tags fastened to the collar give important information—the dog's name, the owner's name, the owner's address and a telephone number where the owner can be reached. This makes it easy for whomever finds the dog to contact the owner and arrange to have the dog returned. An added advantage is that a person will be more likely to approach a lost dog who has ID tags on his collar; it tells the person that this is somebody's pet rather than a stray. This is the easiest and fastest method of identification, provided that the tags stay on the collar and the collar stays on the dog.

Proper ID is essential for your Yorkie at all times, but especially when on a family vacation.

accommodations ahead of time anyway, but this is especially important when traveling with a dog. You do not want to make an overnight stop at the only place around for miles to find out that they do not allow dogs. Also, you do not want to reserve a place for your family without mentioning that you are bringing a dog, because, if it is against their policy, you may not have a place to stay.

Alternatively, if you are traveling and choose not to bring your Yorkshire Terrier, you will have to make arrangements for him while you are away. Some options are to bring him to a neighbor's house to stay while you are gone, to have a trusted neighbor stay at your house or to bring your dog to a reputable boarding kennel. If you choose to board him at a kennel, you should stop by to see the

A typical Yorkie carrying-crate is very satisfactory for the car ride or visit to the vet. This crate is not acceptable for airline travel.

Your Yorkie should always wear his buckle collar to which his dog tags are attached.

facility and where the dogs are kept to make sure that it is clean. Talk to some of the employees and see how they treat the dogs— do they spend time with the dogs, play with them, exercise them, groom them? Do they have experience with small dogs? You know that your Yorkshire Terrier will not be happy unless he gets regular attention. Also find out the kennel's policy on vaccinations and what they require. This is for all of the dogs' safety, since when dogs are kept together, there is a greater risk of diseases being passed from dog to dog. Many vets offer boarding facilities; this is another handy option.

IDENTIFICATION

Your Yorkshire Terrier is your valued companion and friend. That is why you always keep a close eye on him and you have made sure that he cannot escape from the yard or wriggle out of his collar and run away from you. However, accidents can happen and there may come a time when your dog unexpectedly gets separated from you. If this unfortunate event should occur, the first thing on your mind will be finding him. Preventative measures pay off dearly! Proper identification will increase the chances of his being returned to you safely and quickly.

Training Your Yorkshire Terrier

Living with an untrained dog is a lot like owning a piano that you do not know how to play—it is a nice object to look at, but it does not do much more than that to bring you pleasure. Now try taking piano lessons, and suddenly the piano comes alive and brings forth magical sounds and rhythms that set your heart singing and your body swaying.

The same is true with your Yorkshire Terrier. At first you enjoy seeing him around the house. He does not do much with you other than to need attention, grooming, food, water and exercise. Come to think of it, he does not bring you much joy, either. He is a big responsibility with a very small return. And often, he develops unacceptable behaviors that annoy you—to say nothing of bad habits that may end up costing you great sums of money. Not a good thing!

Now train your Yorkshire Terrier. Enroll in an obedience class. Teach him good manners as you learn how and why he behaves the way he does. Find out how to communicate with your dog and how to recognize and understand his communications with you. Suddenly the dog takes on a new role in your life—he is smart, interesting, well behaved and fun to be with, and he demonstrates his bond of devotion to you daily. In other words, your Yorkshire Terrier does wonders for your ego because he constantly reminds you that you are not only his

FAMILY TIES

If you have other pets in the home and/or interact often with the pets of friends and other family members, your dog will respond to those pets in much the same manner as you do. It is only when you show fear of or resentment toward another animal that he will act fearful or unfriendly.

leader, you are his hero! Miraculous things have happened—you have a wonderful dog (even your family and friends have noticed the transformation!) and you feel good about yourself.

Those involved with teaching dog obedience and counseling owners about their dogs' behavior have discovered some interesting facts about dog ownership. For example, training dogs when they are puppies results in the highest rate of success in developing well-mannered and well-adjusted adult dogs. Training an older dog, say from six months to six years of age, can produce almost equal results, providing that the owner accepts the dog's slower rate of learning capability and is willing to work patiently to help the dog succeed at developing to his fullest potential. Unfortunately, the patience factor is what many owners of untrained adult dogs lack, so

they do not persist until their dogs are successful at learning particular behaviors.

Training a puppy, for example, aged 8 to 16 weeks (20 weeks at the most), is like working with a dry sponge in a pool of water. The pup soaks up whatever you show him and constantly looks for more things to do and learn. At this early age, his body is not yet producing hormones, and therein lies the reason for such a high rate of success. Without hormones, he is focused on his owners and not particularly interested in investigating other places, dogs, people, etc. You are his leader: his provider of food, water, shelter and security. Therefore, he latches onto you and wants to stay close. He will usually follow you from room to room, will not let you out of his sight when you are outdoors with him and will respond in like manner to the people and animals you encounter. If, for example, you greet a friend warmly, he will be happy to greet the person as well. If, however, you are hesitant or anxious about the approach of a stranger, he will respond accordingly.

Once the puppy begins to produce hormones, his natural curiosity emerges and he begins to investigate the world around him. It is at that time when you may notice that the untrained

Adolescent Yorkies are as curious. Their hormonal changes inspire them to investigate every scent around them.

dog begins to wander away from you and even ignore your commands to stay close. When this behavior becomes a problem, the owner has two choices: get rid of the dog or train him. It is strongly urged that you choose the latter option.

Occasionally there are no classes available within a reasonable distance from the owner's home. Sometimes there are classes available but the tuition is too costly. Whatever the circumstances, the solution to training your Yorkie without obedience classes lies within the pages of this book. This chapter is devoted to helping you train your Yorkshire Terrier at home. If the recommended procedures are followed faithfully, you may expect positive results that will prove rewarding to both you and your dog.

Whether your Yorkshire Terrier is a puppy or a mature adult, the methods of teaching

Part of housebreaking is training your Yorkie to always use the same relief spot. This should not be a problem, as dogs learn to recognize their chosen sites and return there on their own.

and the techniques we use in training basic behaviors are the same. After all, no dog, whether puppy or adult, likes harsh or inhumane methods. All creatures, however, respond favorably to gentle motivational methods and sincere praise and encouragement. Now let us get started.

HOUSEBREAKING

You can train a puppy to relieve himself wherever you choose. For example, city dwellers often train their puppies to relieve themselves at the curbside because large plots of grass are not readily available. Suburbanites, on the other hand, usually have yards to accommodate their dogs' needs.

Outdoor training includes such surfaces as grass, dirt and cement. Indoor training usually means training your dog to newspaper.

MEALTIME
Mealtime should be a peaceful time for your puppy. Do not put his food and water bowls in a high-traffic area in the house. For example, give him his own little corner of the kitchen where he can eat undisturbed and where he will not be underfoot. Do not allow small children or other family members to disturb the pup when he is eating.

Some Yorkies like stairs, other are afraid of them. Puppies especially cannot use stairs, so a ramp can be helpful if your home is elevated.

When deciding on the surface and location that you will want your Yorkshire Terrier to use, be sure it is going to be permanent. Training your dog to grass and then changing your mind two months later is extremely difficult for both dog and owner.

Next, choose the command you will use each and every time you want your puppy to void. "Go hurry up" and "Go make" are examples of commands commonly used by dog owners. Get in the habit of asking the puppy, "Do you want to go hurry up?" (or whatever your chosen relief command is) before you take him out. That way, when he becomes an adult, you will be able to determine if he wants to go out when you ask him. A confirmation will be signs of interest, such as wagging his tail, watching you intently, going to the door, etc.

PUPPY'S NEEDS

The puppy needs to relieve himself after play periods, after each meal, after he has been sleeping and any time he indicates that he is looking for a place to urinate or defecate. The urinary and intestinal tract muscles of very young puppies are not fully developed. Therefore, like human babies, puppies need to relieve themselves frequently.

Take your puppy out often—every hour for an eight-week-old, for example. The older the puppy, the less often he will need to relieve himself. Finally, as a mature healthy adult, he will require only three to five relief trips per day.

HOUSING AND CONTROL

Since the types of housing and control you provide for your

THE CLEAN LIFE

By providing sleeping and resting quarters that fit the dog, and offering frequent opportunities to relieve himself outside his quarters, the puppy quickly learns that the outdoors (or the newspaper if you are training him to paper) is the place to go when he needs to urinate or defecate. It also reinforces his innate desire to keep his sleeping quarters clean. This, in turn, helps develop the muscle control that will eventually produce a dog with clean living habits.

HOW MANY TIMES A DAY?

AGE	RELIEF TRIPS
To 14 weeks	10
14–22 weeks	8
22–32 weeks	6
Adulthood	4
(dog stops growing)	

These are estimates, of course, but they are a guide to the *minimum* number of opportunities a dog should have each day to relieve himself.

A dog crate is absolutely necessary in the life and training of your Yorkie.

puppy have a direct relationship on the success of house-training, we consider the various aspects of both before we begin training. Bringing a new puppy home and turning him loose in your house can be compared to turning a child loose in a sports arena and telling the child that the place is all his! The sheer enormity of the place would be too much for him to handle. Instead, offer the puppy clearly defined areas where he can play, sleep, eat and live. A room of the house where the family gathers is the most obvious choice. Puppies are social animals and need to feel a part of the pack right from the start. Hearing your voice, watching you while you are doing things and smelling you nearby are all positive reinforcers that he is now a member of your pack. Usually a family room, the kitchen or a nearby adjoining breakfast area is ideal for providing safety and security for both puppy and owner.

Within that room, there should be a smaller area that the puppy can call his own. A wire or fiberglass dog crate or a gated corner from which he can view the activities of his new family will be fine. The size of the area or crate is the key factor here.

Every Yorkie puppy must have a place to call his own. Pet shops have many kinds of dog beds to offer you.

The area must be large enough for the puppy to lay down and stretch out as well as stand up and turn around, yet small enough so that he cannot relieve himself at one end and sleep at the other without coming into contact with his droppings. Dogs are, by nature, clean animals and will not remain close to their relief areas unless forced to do so. In those cases, they then become dirty dogs and usually remain that way for life.

The crate should be lined with a clean towel and offer one toy, no more. Do not put food or water in the crate, as eating and drinking will activate his digestive processes and ultimately defeat your purpose as well as make the puppy very uncomfortable as he attempts to "hold it."

BE CONSISTENT

Most of all, be consistent. Always take your dog to the same location, always use the same command and always have the dog on leash when he is in his relief area, unless a fenced-in yard is available.

By following the Success Method, your puppy will be completely housebroken by the time his muscle and brain development reach maturity. Keep in mind that small breeds usually mature faster than large breeds, but all puppies should be trained by six months of age.

By *control*, we mean helping the puppy to create a lifestyle pattern that will be compatible to that of his human pack (*you*!). Just as we guide little children to learn our way of life, we must show the puppy when it is time to play, eat, sleep, exercise and even entertain himself.

Your puppy should always sleep in his crate. He should also learn that, during times of household confusion and excessive human activity such as at breakfast when family members are preparing for the day, he can play by himself in relative safety and comfort in his crate. Each time you leave the puppy alone, he should be crated. Puppies are chewers. They cannot tell the difference between lamp cords, television wires, shoes, table legs, etc. Chewing into a television wire, for example, can be fatal to the puppy, while a shorted wire can start a fire in the house.

If the puppy chews on the arm of the chair when he is alone, you will probably discipline him angrily when you get home. Thus, he makes the association that your coming home means he is going to be scolded. (He will not remember chewing the chair and is incapable of making the association of the discipline with his naughty deed.)

Canine Development Schedule

It is important to understand how and at what age a puppy develops into adulthood. If you are a puppy owner, consult the following Canine Development Schedule to determine the stage of development your Yorkshire Terrier puppy is currently experiencing. This knowledge will help you as you work with the puppy in the weeks and months ahead.

Period	Age	Characteristics
FIRST TO THIRD	BIRTH TO SEVEN WEEKS	Puppy needs food, sleep and warmth, and responds to simple and gentle touching. Needs mother for security and disciplining. Needs littermates for learning and interacting with other dogs. Pup learns to function within a pack and learns pack order of dominance. Begin socializing pup with adults and children for short periods. Pup begins to become aware of his environment.
FOURTH	EIGHT TO TWELVE WEEKS	Brain is fully developed. Needs socializing with outside world. Remove from mother and littermates. Needs to change from canine pack to human pack. Human dominance necessary. Fear period occurs between 8 and 16 weeks. Avoid fright and pain.
FIFTH	THIRTEEN TO SIXTEEN WEEKS	Training and formal obedience should begin. Less association with other dogs, more with people, places, situations. Period will pass easily if you remember this is pup's change-to-adolescence time. Be firm and fair. Flight instinct prominent. Permissiveness and over-disciplining can do permanent damage. Praise for good behavior.
JUVENILE	FOUR TO EIGHT MONTHS	Another fear period about 7 to 8 months of age. It passes quickly, but be cautious of fright and pain. Sexual maturity reached. Dominant traits established. Dog should understand sit, down, come and stay by now.

NOTE: THESE ARE APPROXIMATE TIME FRAMES. ALLOW FOR INDIVIDUAL DIFFERENCES IN PUPPIES.

Times of excitement, such as family parties, visits, etc., can be fun for the puppy, providing he can view the activities from the security of his crate. He is not underfoot and he is not being fed all sorts of tidbits that will probably cause him stomach distress, yet he still feels a part of the fun.

SCHEDULE

As stated earlier, a puppy should be taken to his relief area each time he is released from his crate, after meals, after play sessions, when he first awakens in the morning (at age eight weeks, this can mean 5 a.m.!) and whenever he indicates by circling or sniffing busily that he needs to urinate or

THE SUCCESS METHOD

6 Steps to Successful Crate Training

1 Tell the puppy "Crate time!" and place him in the crate with a small treat (a piece of cheese or half of a biscuit). Let him stay in the crate for five minutes while you are in the same room. Then release him and praise lavishly. Never release him when he is fussing. Wait until he is quiet before you let him out.

2 Repeat Step 1 several times a day.

3 The next day, place the puppy in the crate as before. Let him stay there for ten minutes. Do this several times.

4 Continue building time in five-minute increments until the puppy stays in his crate for 30 minutes with you in the room. Always take him to his relief area after prolonged periods in his crate.

5 Now go back to Step 1 and let the puppy stay in his crate for five minutes, this time while you are out of the room.

6 Once again, build crate time in five-minute increments with you out of the room. When the puppy will stay willingly in his crate (he may even fall asleep!) for 30 minutes with you out of the room, he will be ready to stay in it for several hours at a time.

A dog uses his crate as a place away from it all. The crate door should always be open when the dog is not in residence.

defecate. For a puppy less than ten weeks of age, a routine of taking him out every hour is necessary. As the puppy grows, he will be able to wait for longer periods of time.

Keep trips to his relief area short. Stay no more than five or six minutes and then return to the house. If he goes during that time, praise him lavishly and take him indoors immediately. If he does not, but he has an accident when you go back indoors, pick him up immediately, say "No! No!" and return to his relief area. Wait a few minutes, then return to the house again. *Never* hit a puppy or put his face in urine or excrement when he has an accident!

Once indoors, put the puppy

in his crate until you have had time to clean up his accident. Then release him to the family area and watch him more closely than before. Chances are, his accident was a result of your not picking up his signal or waiting too long before offering him the opportunity to relieve himself. *Never* hold a grudge against the puppy for accidents.

Let the puppy learn that going outdoors means it is time to relieve himself, not play. Once trained, he will be able to play indoors and out and still differentiate between the times for play versus the times for relief.

Help him develop regular hours for naps, being alone, playing by himself and just rest-

For traveling, two dogs per crate is okay; the dogs may enjoy each other's company. In the home, though, it's one dog per crate so that each dog has his own personal space.

ing, all in his crate. Encourage him to entertain himself while you are busy with your activities. Let him learn that having you near is comforting, but it is not your main purpose in life to provide him with undivided attention.

THE SUCCESS METHOD

Success that comes by luck is usually short-lived. Success that comes by well-thought-out proven methods is often more easily achieved and permanent. This is the Success Method. It is designed to give you, the puppy owner, a simple yet proven way to help your puppy develop clean living habits and a feeling of security in his new environment.

Each time you put a puppy in his crate tell him, "Crate time!" (or whatever command you choose). Soon, he will run to his crate when he hears you say those words. In the beginning of his training, do not leave him in his crate for prolonged periods of time except during the night when everyone is sleeping. Make his experience with his crate a pleasant one and, as an adult, he will love his crate and willingly stay in it for several hours. There are millions of people who go to work every day and leave their adult dogs crated while they are away. The dogs accept this as their lifestyle and look forward to "crate time."

Crate training provides safety for you, the puppy and the home. It also provides the puppy with a feeling of security, and that helps the puppy achieve self-confidence and clean habits. Remember that one of the primary ingredients in house-training your puppy is control. Regardless of your lifestyle, there will always be occasions when you will need to have a place where your dog can stay and be happy and safe. Crate training is the answer for now and in the future.

In conclusion, a few key elements are really all you need for a successful house- and crate-training method—consistency, frequency, praise, control and supervision. By following these procedures with a normal, healthy puppy, you and the puppy will soon be past the stage of "accidents" and ready to move on to a full and rewarding life together.

DISCIPLINE, REWARD AND PUNISHMENT

Discipline, training one to act in accordance with rules, brings order to life. It is as simple as that. Without discipline, particularly in a group society, chaos reigns supreme and the group will eventually perish. Humans and canines are social animals and need some form of discipline in order to function effectively. They must procure food, reproduce to keep the species going and protect their home base and their young. If there were no discipline in the lives of social animals, they would eventually die from starvation and/or predation by other

PAPER CAPER
Never line your pup's sleeping area with newspaper. Puppy litters are usually raised on newspaper and, once in your home, the puppy will immediately associate newspaper with voiding. Never put newspaper on any floor while house-training, as this will only confuse the puppy. If you are paper-training him, use paper in his designated relief area only. Finally, restrict water intake after evening meals. Offer a few licks at a time—never let a young puppy gulp water after meals.

stronger animals. In the case of domestic canines, dogs need discipline in their lives in order to understand how their pack (you and other family members) functions and how they must act in order to survive.

A large humane society in a highly populated area recently surveyed dog owners regarding their satisfaction with their relationships with their dogs. People who had trained their dogs were 75% more satisfied with their pets than those who had never trained their dogs.

Dr. Edward Thorndike, a well-known psychologist, established *Thorndike's Theory of Learning*, which states that a behavior that results in a pleasant event tends to be repeated. Likewise, a behavior that results in an unpleasant event tends not to be repeated. It is this theory on which training methods are based today. For example, if you manipulate a dog to perform a specific behavior and reward him for doing it, he is likely to do it again because he enjoyed the end result.

Occasionally, punishment, a penalty inflicted for an offense, is necessary. The best type of punishment often comes from an outside source. For example, a child is told not to touch the stove because he may get burned. He disobeys and touches the stove. In doing so, he receives a burn. From that time on, he respects the heat of the stove and avoids contact with it. Therefore, a behavior that results in an unpleasant event tends not to be repeated.

A good example of a dog learning the hard way is the dog who chases the house cat. He is told many times to leave the cat alone, yet he persists in teasing

Yorkies are among the most portable of all dogs. Many Yorkie owners like their dogs to accompany them whenever possible, and the feeling is mutual!

> **PLAN TO PLAY**
> The puppy should also have regular play and exercise sessions when he is with you or a family member. Exercise for a very young puppy can consist of a short walk around the house or yard. Playing can include fetching games with a large ball or a special toy. (All puppies teethe and need soft things upon which to chew.) Remember to restrict play periods to indoors within his living area (the family room, for example) until he is completely house-trained.

the cat. Then, one day he begins chasing the cat but the cat turns and swipes a claw across the dog's face, leaving him with a painful gash on his nose. The final result is that the dog stops chasing the cat.

TRAINING EQUIPMENT

COLLAR
For most Yorkies, the basic buckle collar, usually constructed of nylon or cotton, is ideal. The best quality collars can be purchased at a local pet shop, where a wide selection of colors and styles are available.

LEASH
A 3- to 6-foot leash is recommended, preferably made of leather, nylon or heavy cloth. A lightweight leash is the best choice for the Yorkie.

CHOOSE AN APPROPRIATE COLLAR

The **BUCKLE COLLAR** is the standard collar used for everyday purposes. Be sure that you adjust the buckle on growing puppies. Check it every day. It can become too tight overnight! These collars can be made of leather or nylon. Attach your dog's identification tags to this collar.

The **CHOKE COLLAR** is designed for training. It is constructed of highly polished steel so that it slides easily through the stainless steel loop. The idea is that the dog controls the pressure around its neck and he will stop pulling if the collar becomes uncomfortable. It is not suitable for small dogs or long-coated dogs, and should *never* be used on a Yorkie.

The **HALTER** is for a trained dog that has to be restrained to prevent running away, chasing a cat and the like. Considered the most humane of all collars, it is frequently used on smaller dogs on which collars are not comfortable.

Yorkies quickly learn about treats and will react when a treat is offered. Remember that a treat is a reward, so be wise about when you offer treats.

TREATS

Have a bag of treats on hand. Something nutritious and easy to swallow works best; use a soft treat, a slice of cheese or a piece of cooked chicken rather than a dry biscuit. By the time the dog gets done chewing a dry treat, he will forget why he is being rewarded in the first place! By the way, using food rewards will not teach a dog to beg at the table—the only way to teach a dog to beg at the table is to give him food from the table. In training, rewarding the dog with a food treat away from the table will help him associate praise and the treats with learning new behaviors that obviously please his owner.

TRAINING BEGINS: ASK THE DOG A QUESTION

In order to teach your dog anything, you must first get his attention. After all, he cannot learn anything if he is looking away from you with his mind on something else. To get his attention, ask him "School?" and immediately walk over to him and give him a treat as you tell him "Good dog." Wait a minute or two and repeat the routine, this time with a treat in your hand as you approach the dog to within a foot of him. Do not go directly to him, but stop about a foot short of him and hold out the treat as you ask "School?" He will see you approaching with a treat in your hand and most likely begin walking toward you. As you meet, give him the treat and praise again.

The third time, ask the question, have a treat in your hand and walk only a short distance

TRAINING RULES

If you want to be successful in training your dog, you have four rules to obey yourself:
1. Develop an understanding of how a dog thinks.
2. Do not blame the dog for lack of communication.
3. Define your dog's personality and act accordingly.
4. Have patience and be consistent.

THE BASIC COMMANDS

TEACHING SIT

Now that you have the dog's attention, hold the leash in your left hand and the food treat in your right. Place your food hand at the dog's nose and let him lick the treat but not take it from you. Say "Sit" and slowly raise your food hand from in front of the dog's nose up over his head so that he is looking at the ceiling. As he bends his head upward, he will have to bend his knees to maintain his

toward the dog so that he must walk almost all the way to you. As he reaches you, give him the treat and praise again.

By this time, the dog will probably be getting the idea that if he pays attention to you, especially when you ask that question, it will pay off in treats and fun activities for him. In other words, he learns that "school" means doing fun things with you that result in treats and positive attention for him.

Remember that the dog does not understand your verbal language, he only recognizes sounds. Your question translates to a series of sounds for him, and those sounds become the signal to go to you and pay attention; if he does, he will get to interact with you plus receive treats and praise.

Training should begin while the Yorkie is still a puppy. Dogs must learn that certain behavior is expected, and that other behavior is unacceptable.

balance. As he bends his knees, he will assume a sit position. At that point, release the food treat and praise lavishly with comments such as "Good dog! Good sit!," etc. Remember to always praise enthusiastically, because dogs relish verbal praise from their owners and feel so proud of themselves whenever they accomplish a behavior.

You will not use food forever in getting the dog to obey your commands. Food is only used to teach new behav-iors, and once the dog knows what you want when you give a specific command, you will wean him off the food treats but still maintain the verbal praise. After all, you will always have your voice with you, but there will be many times when you have no food rewards yet you expect the dog to obey.

TEACHING DOWN

Teaching the down exercise is easy when you understand how the dog perceives the down position, but it is very difficult when you do not. In addition, teaching the down exercise using a forceful method can sometimes make the dog develop such a fear of the down that he either runs away when you say "Down" or he attempts to bite the person who tries to force him down.

Have the dog sit close alongside your left leg, facing in the same direction as you are. Hold the leash in your left hand and a food treat in your right. Now place your left hand lightly on the top of the dog's shoulders where they meet above the spinal cord. Do not push down on the dog's shoulders; simply rest your left hand there so you can guide the dog to lie down close to your left leg rather than to swing away from your side when he drops.

Now place the food hand at

DOUBLE JEOPARDY

A dog in jeopardy never lies down. He stays alert on his feet because instinct tells him that he may have to run away or fight for his survival. Therefore, if a dog feels threatened or anxious, he will not lie down. Consequently, it is important to keep the dog calm and relaxed as he learns the down exercise.

the dog's nose, say "Down" very softly (almost a whisper) and slowly lower the food hand to the dog's front feet. When the food hand reaches the floor, begin moving it forward along the floor in front of the dog. Keep talking softly to the dog, saying things like, "Do you want this treat? You can do this, good dog." Your reassuring tone of voice will help calm the dog as he tries to follow the food hand in order to get the treat.

When the dog's elbows touch the floor, release the food and praise softly. Try to get the dog to maintain that down position for several seconds before you let him sit up again. The goal here is to get the dog to

PRACTICE MAKES PERFECT!
- Have training lessons with your dog every day in several short segments—three to five times a day for a few minutes at a time is ideal.
- Do not have long practice sessions. The dog will become easily bored.
- Never practice when you are tired, ill, worried or in an otherwise negative mood. This will transmit to the dog and may have an adverse effect on his performance.

Think fun, short and above all *positive*! End each session on a high note, rather than a failed exercise, and make sure to give a lot of praise. Enjoy the training and help your dog enjoy it, too.

settle down and not feel threatened in the down position.

TEACHING STAY
It is easy to teach the dog to stay in either a sit or a down position. Again, we use food and praise during the teaching process as we help the dog to understand exactly what it is that we are expecting him to do.

To teach the sit/stay, start with the dog sitting on your left side as before and hold the leash in your left hand. Have a food treat in your right hand and place your food hand at the dog's nose. Say "Stay" and step out on your right foot to stand directly in front of the dog, toe to toe, as he licks and nibbles the treat. Be sure to keep his head facing upward to maintain the sit position. Count to five and then swing around to stand next to the dog again with him on your left. As soon as you get back to the original position,

The owner practices the down/stay with hand signals, while keeping his foot on the leash so that the dog is secure and cannot run off.

CALM DOWN

Dogs will do anything for your attention. If you reward the dog when he is calm and resting, you will develop a well-mannered dog. If, on the other hand, you greet your dog excitedly and encourage him to wrestle with you, the dog will greet you the same way and you will have a hyperactive dog on your hands.

release the food and praise lavishly.

To teach the down/stay, do the down as previously described. As soon as the dog lies down, say "Stay" and step out on your right foot just as you did in the sit/stay. Count to five and then return to stand beside the dog with him on your left side. Release the treat and praise as always.

Within a week or ten days, you can begin to add a bit of distance between you and your

dog when you leave him. When you do, use your left hand open with the palm facing the dog as a stay signal, much the same as the hand signal a police officer uses to stop traffic at an intersection. Hold the food treat in your right hand as before, but this time the food is not touching the dog's nose. He will watch the food hand and quickly learn that he is going to get that treat as soon as you return to his side.

When you can stand 3 feet away from your dog for 30 seconds, you can then begin building time and distance in both stays. Eventually, the dog can be expected to remain in the stay position for prolonged periods of time until you return to him or call him to you. Always praise lavishly when he stays.

TEACHING COME

If you make teaching "come" a fun experience, you should never have a student that does not love the game or that fails to come when called. The secret, it seems, is never to teach the word "come."

At times when an owner most wants his dog to come when called, the owner is likely upset or anxious and he allows these feelings to come through in the tone of his voice when he calls his dog. Hearing that desperation in his owner's

Once you get your Yorkie to sit and stay, you can begin to build time and distance into the discipline and stand further away for a longer period of time.

voice, the dog fears the results of going to him and therefore either disobeys outright or runs in the opposite direction. The secret, therefore, is to teach the dog a game and, when you want him to come to you, simply play the game. It is practically a no-fail solution!

To begin, have several members of your family take a few food treats and each go into a different room in the house. Take turns calling the dog, and each person should celebrate the dog's finding him with a treat and lots of happy praise. When a person calls the dog, he is actually inviting the dog to find him and get a treat as a reward for "winning."

A few turns of the "Where are you?" game and the dog will figure out that everyone is playing the game and that each person has a big celebration awaiting his success at locating them. Once he learns to love the game, simply calling out "Where are you?" will bring him running from wherever he is when he hears that all-important question.

The come command is recognized as one of the most important things to teach a dog, so it is interesting to note that there are trainers who work with thousands of dogs and never teach the actual word "come." Yet these dogs will race to respond to a person who uses the dog's name followed by "Where are you?" In one instance, for example, a woman has a 12-year-old companion dog who went blind, but who never fails to locate her owner when asked "Where are you?"

Children particularly love to play this game with their dogs. Children can hide in smaller places like a shower or bathtub, behind a bed or under a table. The dog needs to work a little bit harder to find these hiding places, but, when he does, he loves to celebrate with a treat and a tussle with a favorite youngster.

TUG OF WALK?

If you begin teaching the heel by taking long walks and letting the dog pull you along, he misinterprets this action as an acceptable form of taking a walk. When you pull back on the leash to counteract his pulling, he reads that tug as a signal to pull even harder!

In order for a Yorkshire Terrier to succeed in the show ring, the dog must master the heel command. Proper gaiting requires the dog to move easily at his master's side.

TEACHING HEEL

Heeling means that the dog walks beside the owner without pulling. It takes time and patience on the owner's part to succeed at teaching the dog that he (the owner) will not proceed unless the dog is walking calmly beside him. Pulling out ahead on the leash is definitely not acceptable.

Begin with holding the leash in your left hand as the dog sits beside your left leg. Hold the

Always teach and practice commands with the dog on leash. Once commands have been learned reliably and you want to practice off-leash, only do so in a securely fenced area.

loop end of the leash in your right hand but keep your left hand short on the leash so it keeps the dog in close next to you. Say "Heel" and step forward on your left foot. Keep the dog close to you and take three steps. Stop and have the dog sit next to you in what we now call the heel position. Praise verbally, but do not touch the dog. Hesitate a moment and begin again with "Heel," taking three steps and stopping, at which point the dog is told to sit again.

Your goal here is to have the dog walk those three steps without pulling on the leash. When he will walk calmly beside you for three steps without pulling, increase the number of steps you take to five. When he will walk politely beside you while you take five steps, you can increase the length of your walk to ten steps. Keep increasing the length of your stroll until the dog will walk quietly beside you without pulling as long as you want him to heel. When you stop heeling, indicate to the dog that the exercise is over by verbally praising as you pet him and say "OK, good dog." The "OK" is used as a release word, meaning that the exercise is finished and the dog is free to relax.

If you are dealing with a dog who insists on pulling you

around, simply "put on your brakes" and stand your ground until the dog realizes that the two of you are not going anywhere until he is beside you and moving at your pace, not his. It may take some time just standing there to convince the dog that you are the leader and you will be the one to decide on the direction and speed of your travel.

Each time the dog looks up at you or slows down to give a slack leash between the two of you, quietly praise him and say, "Good heel. Good dog." Eventu-

REAP THE REWARDS

If you start with a normal, healthy dog and give him time, patience and some carefully executed lessons, you will reap the rewards of that training for the life of the dog. And what a life it will be! The two of you will find immeasurable pleasure in the companionship you have built together with love, respect and under-standing.

ally, the dog will begin to respond and within a few days he will be walking politely beside you without pulling on the leash. At first, the training sessions should be kept short and very positive; soon the dog will be able to walk nicely with you for increasingly longer distances. Remember also to give the dog free time and the opportunity to run and play when you are done with heel practice.

When you stop walking, a properly trained Yorkie will stop and await your next command.

WEANING OFF FOOD IN TRAINING

Food is used in training new behaviors, yet once the dog understands what behavior goes with a specific command, it is time to start weaning him off the food treats. At first, give a treat after each exercise. Then, start to give a treat only after every other exercise. Mix up the

OBEDIENCE CLASSES

As previously discussed, it is a good idea to enroll in an obedience class if one is available in your area. If yours is a show dog, handling classes are a smart choice. Many areas have dog clubs that offer basic obedience training as well as preparatory classes for obedience competition. There are also local dog trainers who offer similar classes.

At obedience trials, dogs can earn titles at various levels of competition. The beginning levels of competition include basic behaviors such as sit, down, heel, etc. The more advanced levels of competition include jumping, retrieving, scent discrimination and signal work. The advanced levels require a dog and owner to put a lot of time and effort into their

Using food rewards, most trainers agree, is the easiest way to train a dog. Yorkies, like most other dogs, respond positively to this routine bribery!

times when you offer a food reward and the times when you only offer praise so that the dog will never know when he is going to receive both food and praise and when he is going to receive only praise. This is called a variable ratio reward system and it proves successful because there is always the chance that the owner will produce a treat, so the dog never stops trying for that reward. No matter what, *always* give verbal praise.

A BORN PRODIGY

Occasionally, a dog and owner who have not attended formal classes have been able to earn entry-level titles by obtaining competition rules and regulations from a local kennel club and practicing on their own to a degree of perfection. Obtaining the higher level titles, however, almost always requires extensive training under the tutelage of experienced instructors. In addition, the more difficult levels require more specialized equipment whereas the lower levels do not.

....and you thought a Yorkie was only a lap dog. Yorkies can compete in advanced levels of obedience training. With patience and consistency, the Yorkie can be trained to do almost anything!

training; the titles that can be earned at these levels of competition are very prestigious.

OTHER ACTIVITIES FOR LIFE

Whether a dog is trained in the structured environment of a class or alone with his owner at home, there are many activities that can bring fun and rewards to both owner and dog once they have mastered basic control.

Teaching the dog to help out around the home, in the yard or on the farm provides great satisfaction to both dog and owner. In addition, the dog's help makes life a little easier for his owner and raises his stature as a valued companion to his family.

It helps give the dog a purpose; it helps to keep his mind occupied and provides an outlet for his energy.

If you are interested in participating in organized competition with your Yorkshire Terrier, there are other activities other than obedience in which

THINK BEFORE YOU BARK
Dogs are sensitive to their masters' moods and emotions. Use your voice wisely when communicating with your dog. Never raise your voice at your dog unless you are trying to correct him. Remember, "barking" at your dog can become as meaningless to him as "dogs-peak" is to you.

you and your dog can become involved. Agility is a popular and fun sport where dogs run through an obstacle course that includes various jumps, tunnels and other exercises to test the dog's speed and coordination. The owners often run through the course beside their dogs to give commands and to guide them through the course. Although competitive, the focus is on fun—it's fun to do and fun to watch, as well as great exercise.

OBEDIENCE SCHOOL

A basic obedience beginner's class usually lasts for six to eight weeks. Dog and owner attend an hour-long lesson once a week and practice for a few minutes, several times a day, each day at home. If done properly, the whole procedure will result in a well-mannered dog and an owner who delights in living with a pet that is eager to please and enjoys doing things with his owner.

Yes, Yorkies are small, but they have tremendous brain power and a strong desire to please. With these characteristics in your arsenal, you should be able to train your dog for agility trials.

Crate training is extremely important in the life of a Yorkie. For the protection of your Yorkie, the crate is the safest refuge. In addition to being the best aid in training and housebreaking, crates are ideal for traveling to a dog show, the vet's office or your vacation destination.

Health Care of Your Yorkshire Terrier

Dogs, being mammals like human beings, suffer from many of the same physical illnesses as people. Since people usually know more about human diseases than canine maladies, many of the terms used in this chapter will be the familiar terms, not necessarily those used by veterinarians. We use the term *x-ray*, instead of the more acceptable term *radiograph*. We will also use the familiar term *symptoms* even though dogs don't have symptoms, dogs have *clinical signs*. Symptoms are actually verbal descriptions of the patient's feelings. Since dogs can't speak,

Select your vet based upon proximity to your home and recommendations from other dog owners.

> **PARVO FOR THE COURSE**
> Canine parvovirus is a highly contagious disease that attacks puppies and older dogs. Spread through contact with infected feces, parvovirus causes bloody diarrhea, vomiting, heart damage, dehydration, shock and death. To prevent this tragedy, have your puppy begin his series of vaccinations at six to eight weeks of age. Be aware that the virus is easily spread and is carried on a dog's hair, feet, water bowls and other objects, as well as on people's shoes and clothing.

we have to look for clinical signs...but we still use the term *symptoms* in this book.

As a general rule, medicine is *practiced*. Medicine is a constantly changing art as we learn more and more about genetics, electronic aids (like CAT scans and MRIs) and daily laboratory advances. There are many dog maladies, like hip dysplasia, which are not universally treated in the same manner. Some veterinarians opt for surgery more often than others.

A SKUNKY PROBLEM

Have you noticed your dog dragging his rump along the floor? If so, it is likely that his anal sacs are impacted or possibly infected. The anal sacs are small pouches located on both sides of the anus under the skin and muscles. They are about the size and shape of a grape and contain a foul-smelling liquid. Their contents are usually emptied when the dog has a bowel movement but, if not emptied completely, they will impact, which will cause your dog much pain. Fortunately, your veterinarian can tend to this problem easily by draining the sacs for the dog. Be aware that your dog might also empty his anal sacs in cases of extreme fright.

Your vet will give your puppy a thorough examination as soon as you get him as possible. If there is a medical problem, it should be treated immediately and the breeder should be notified.

SELECTING A QUALIFIED VET

Your selection of a vet should be based upon his personality and skills with small dogs as well as his convenience to your home. You want a vet who is close as you might have emergencies or multiple visits for treatments. You want a vet who has services that you might require such as boarding and grooming facilities, who makes sophisticated pet supplies available and who has a good reputation for ability and responsiveness. There is nothing more frustrating than having to wait a day or more to get a response from a veterinarian.

All veterinarians are licensed and their diplomas and/or certificates should be displayed in their waiting rooms. There are, however, many veterinary specialties that usually require further studies and internships. There are specialists in heart problems (veterinary cardiologists), skin problems (veterinary dermatologists), teeth and gum problems (veterinary dentists), eye problems

A typical vet's income, categorized according to services performed. This survey dealt with small-animal (pets) practices.

Breakdown of Veterinary Income by Category

2%	Dentistry
4%	Radiology
12%	Surgery
15%	Vaccinations
19%	Laboratory
23%	Examinations
25%	Medicines

MEDICAL PROBLEMS
MOST FREQUENTLY SEEN IN YORKSHIRE TERRIERS

Condition	Age Affected	Cause	Area Affected
Cataracts	3 to 6 years	Congenital	Lens of the eyes
Collapsed Trachea	Adult	Possibly congenital or diet	Upper trachea
Cryptorchidism	Birth (by 4 months)	Congenital	Testicle(s)
Elbow Dysplasia	1 to 2 years	Congenital	Elbow joint
Hip Dysplasia	By 2 years	Congenital	Hip joint
Hypoglycemia	First few weeks	Possbily congenital	Blood
Hypothyroidism	1 to 3 years	Lymphocytic thyroiditis	Endocrine system
Keratoconjunctivitis Sicca	Adult	Congenital/immunological	Tear ducts of eyes
Legg-Calve-Perthes Disease	4 to 12 months	Congenital	Leg
Medial Patellar Luxation	Any age	Congenital	Knee cap
Progressive Retinal Atrophy	5 years an older	Congenital	Retinal tissue of eyes
Ulcerative Keratitis	Any age	Irritating hairs (on eyes)	Surface of cornea
Valvular Insufficiency	7 to 8 years	Possibly congenital	Heart valves
Vertebral Malformation	Less than 1 year	Unknown	Spinal cord
Von Willebrand's Disease	Birth	Congenital	Blood

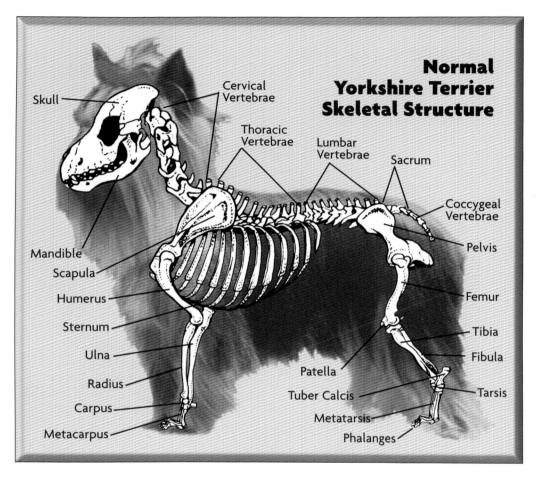

Normal Yorkshire Terrier Skeletal Structure

Skull

Cervical Vertebrae

Thoracic Vertebrae

Lumbar Vertebrae

Sacrum

Coccygeal Vertebrae

Pelvis

Mandible

Scapula

Humerus

Sternum

Ulna

Radius

Carpus

Metacarpus

Femur

Tibia

Fibula

Patella

Tuber Calcis

Metatarsis

Phalanges

Tarsis

MORE THAN VACCINES

Vaccinations help prevent your new puppy from contracting diseases, but they do not cure them. Proper nutrition as well as parasite control keep your dog healthy and less susceptible to many dangerous diseases. Remember that your dog depends on you to ensure his well-being.

(veterinary ophthalmologists) and x-rays (veterinary radiologists), and vets who have specialties in bones, muscles or certain organs. Most vets do routine surgery such as neutering, stitching up wounds and docking tails for those breeds in which such is required for show purposes. When the problem affecting your dog is serious, it is not unusual or impudent to get another medical opinion. You might also want to compare costs between several veterinarians.

Sophisticated health care and veterinary services can be very costly. Don't be shy about discussing these costs with your veterinarian. It is not infrequent that important decisions are based upon financial considerations.

PREVENTATIVE MEDICINE

It is much easier, less costly and more effective to practice preventative medicine than to fight bouts of illness and disease. Properly bred puppies come from parents that were selected based upon their genetic-disease profiles.

PET ADVANTAGES

If you do not intend to show or breed your new puppy, your veterinarian will probably recommend that you spay your female or neuter your male. Some people believe neutering leads to weight gain, but if you feed and exercise your dog properly, this is easily avoided. Spaying or neutering can actually have many positive outcomes, such as:
- training becomes easier, as the dog focuses less on the urge to mate and more on you!
- females are protected from unplanned pregnancy as well as ovarian and uterine cancers.
- males are guarded from testicular tumors and have a reduced risk of developing prostate cancer.

Talk to your vet regarding the right age to spay/neuter and other aspects of the procedure.

Their mothers should have been vaccinated, free of all internal and external parasites and properly nourished. For these reasons, a visit to the veterinarian who cared for the dam is recommended. The dam can pass on disease resistance to her puppies. This resistance can last for eight to ten weeks. She can also pass on parasites and many infections. That's why you should learn as much about the dam's health as possible.

Vaccination Scheduling

Most vaccinations are given by injection and should only be done by a veterinarian. Both he and you should keep a record of the date of the injection, the identification of the vaccine and the amount given. The vaccination scheduling is based on a 15-day cycle. The first vaccinations should start when the puppy is 6–8 weeks old, then 15 days later when he is 10–12 weeks of age and later when he is 14–16 weeks of age. Vaccinations should *never* be given without a 15-day lapse between injections.

Most vaccinations immunize your puppy against viruses. The usual vaccines contain immunizing doses of several different viruses such as distemper, parvovirus, parainfluenza and hepatitis. There are other vaccines available when the puppy is at risk. You should rely upon professional advice. This is especially true for the booster-shot program. Most vaccination programs require a booster when the puppy is a year old, and once a year thereafter. In some cases, circumstances may require more or less frequent immunizations.

Kennel cough, more formally known as tracheobronchitis, is treated with a vaccine which is sprayed into the dog's nostrils.

The effectiveness of a parvovirus vaccination program can be tested to be certain that the vaccinations are protective. Your veterinarian will explain and manage all of these details.

PUPPY WORMING

Caring for the puppy starts before the puppy is born by keeping the dam healthy and well-nourished. When the puppy is about three weeks old, he must start his disease-control regimen. The first treatments will be for worms. Most puppies have worms, even if they are tested negative for worms. The test essentially is checking the stool specimens for the eggs of the worms. The worms continually shed eggs except during their dormant stage, when they just rest in the tissues of the puppy. During this stage they don't shed eggs and are not evident during a routine examination.

HEALTH AND VACCINATION SCHEDULE

Age in Weeks:	6TH	8TH	10TH	12TH	14TH	16TH	20-24TH	52ND
Worm Control	✔	✔	✔	✔	✔	✔	✔	
Neutering								✔
Heartworm		✔		✔		✔	✔	
Parvovirus	✔		✔		✔		✔	✔
Distemper		✔		✔		✔		✔
Hepatitis		✔		✔		✔		✔
Leptospirosis								✔
Parainfluenza	✔		✔		✔			✔
Dental Examination		✔					✔	✔
Complete Physical		✔					✔	✔
Coronavirus				✔			✔	✔
Kennel Cough	✔							
Hip Dysplasia								✔
Rabies							✔	

Vaccinations are not instantly effective. It takes about two weeks for the dog's immune system to develop antibodies. Most vaccinations require annual booster shots. Your veterinarian should guide you in this regard.

WEANING TO FIVE MONTHS OLD

Puppies should be weaned by the time they are about two months old. A puppy that remains for at least eight weeks with his mother and littermates usually adapts better to other dogs and people later in life.

In every case, you should have your newly acquired puppy examined by a veterinarian immediately. Vaccination programs usually begin when the puppy is very young.

The puppy will have his teeth examined, his skeletal conformation checked and his general health checked prior to certification by the vet. Many puppies have problems with their knee caps, cataracts and other eye problems, heart murmurs and undescended testicles. They may also have personality problems and your veterinarian might have training in temperament evaluation.

FIVE MONTHS TO ONE YEAR OF AGE

By the time your puppy is five months old, he should have completed his vaccination program. During his physical examination he should be evaluated for Legg-Calve-Perthes disease plus other diseases of the joints. There are tests to assist in the prediction of these problems. Other tests can also be run, such as the aforementioned parvovirus antibody titer, which can assess

IDENTIFICATION OPTIONS

As puppies become more and more expensive, especially those puppies of high quality for showing and/or breeding, they have a greater chance of being stolen. The usual collar dog tag is, of course, easily removed. But there are two more permanent techniques that have become widely used for identification.

The puppy microchip implantation involves the injection of a small microchip, about the size of a corn kernel, under the skin of the dog. If your dog shows up at a clinic or shelter, or is offered for resale under less-than-savory circumstances, it can be positively identified by the microchip. The microchip is scanned, and a registry quickly identifies you as the owner.

Tattooing is done on various parts of the dog, from his belly to his cheeks. The number tattooed can be your telephone number or any other number that you can easily memorize. When professional dog thieves see a tattooed dog, they usually lose interest. For the safety of our dogs, no laboratory facility or dog broker will accept a tattooed dog as stock.

Discuss microchipping and tattooing with your veterinarian and breeder. Some vets perform these services on their own premises for a reasonable fee. Be certain that the dog do is then properly registered with a legitimate national database in order to ensure the effectiveness of his identification.

the effectiveness of the vaccination program.

Unless you intend to breed or show your dog, neutering the puppy at six months of age is recommended. Discuss this with your veterinarian. If the puppy is not top-class and therefore is not a candidate for the show ring or for a serious breeding program, most professionals advise neutering the puppy. In fact, responsible breeders will require as part of their sales agreements that pet-quality pups be neutered (males) or spayed (females). Neutering and spaying have proven to be extremely bene-

DENTAL HEALTH

A dental examination is in order when the dog is between six months and one year of age so that any permanent teeth that have erupted incorrectly can be corrected. It is important to begin a brushing routine at home, using dental-care products made for dogs, such as a small toothbrush and specially formulated toothpaste. Durable nylon and safe edible chews should be a part of your Yorkie's arsenal for good health, good teeth and pleasant breath. The vast majority of dogs three to four years old and older has diseases of the gums from lack of dental attention. Using the various types of dental chews can be very effective in controlling dental plaque.

ficial to both male and female dogs. Besides the obvious impossibility of pregnancy, it inhibits (but does not prevent) breast cancer in bitches and prostate cancer in male dogs.

Blood tests are performed for heartworm infestation and it is possible that your puppy will be placed on a preventative therapy, which will prevent heartworm infection as well as control other internal parasites.

DOGS OLDER THAN ONE YEAR

Continue to visit the veterinarian at least once a year. There is no such disease as old age, but bodily functions do change with age, and the eyes and ears are no longer as efficient. Neither are the internal workings of the liver, kidneys and intestines. Proper dietary changes, recommended by your veterinarian, can make life more pleasant for the aging Yorkshire Terrier and you.

SKIN PROBLEMS IN YORKSHIRE TERRIERS

Veterinarians are consulted by dog owners for skin problems more than for any other group of diseases or maladies. Dogs' skin is almost as sensitive as human skin and both suffer from almost the same ailments (though the occurrence of acne in most breeds is rare!). For this reason, veterinary dermatology has developed into a specialty practiced by many vets.

Since many skin problems have visual symptoms that are almost identical, it requires the skill of an experienced veterinary dermatologist to identify and cure many of the more severe skin disorders. Pet shops sell many treatments for skin problems. Most of the treatments are simply directed at symptoms and not the underlying problem(s). Simply put, if your dog is suffering from a skin disorder, seek professional assistance as quickly as possible. As with all diseases, the earlier a problem is identified and treated, the more successful can be the cure.

AUTO-IMMUNE SKIN CONDITIONS

Auto-immune skin conditions are commonly referred to as being allergic to yourself. Allergies, though, usually result in inflammatory reactions to an outside stimulus. Auto-immune diseases cause serious damage to the tissues which are involved.

The best known auto-immune disease is lupus. It affects people as well as dogs. The symptoms are very variable and may affect the kidneys, bones, blood chemistry and skin. It can be fatal to both dogs and humans, though it is not thought to be transmissible. It is usually successfully treated with cortisone, prednisone or a similar corticosteroid, but extensive use of these drugs can have harmful side effects.

HEREDITARY SKIN DISORDERS

Veterinary dermatologists are currently researching a number of skin disorders that are believed to have a hereditary basis. These inherited diseases are transmitted by both parents, who appear (phenotypically) normal but have a recessive gene for the disease, meaning that they carry, but are not affected by, the disease. These diseases pose serious problems to breeders because in some instances there are no methods of identifying carriers. Often the secondary diseases associated with these skin conditions are even more debilitating than the skin disorders themselves, including cancers and respiratory problems.

Among the hereditary skin

KNOW WHEN TO POSTPONE A VACCINATION

While the visit to the vet is costly, it is never advisable to update a vaccination when visiting with a sick or pregnant dog. Vaccinations should be avoided for all elderly dogs. If your dog is showing the signs of any illness or any medical condition, no matter how serious or mild, including skin irritations, do not vaccinate. Likewise, a lame dog should never be vaccinated; any dog undergoing surgery or on any immunosuppressant drugs should not be vaccinated until fully recovered.

disorders, for which the mode of inheritance is known, are cutaneous asthenia (Ehlers-Danlos syndrome); sebaceous adenitis; cyclic hematopoiesis; dermatomyositis; IgA deficiency; color dilution alopecia and nodular dermatofibrosis. All inherited diseases must be diagnosed and treated by a veterinary specialist.

Before a single pup is produced, breeders must screen their stock for known hereditary illnesses.

Disease	What is it?	What causes it?	Symptoms
Leptospirosis	Severe disease that affects the internal organs; can be spread to people.	A bacterium, which is often carried by rodents, that enters through mucous membranes and spreads quickly throughout the body.	Range from fever, vomiting and loss of appetite in less severe cases to shock, irreversible kidney damage and possibly death in most severe cases.
Rabies	Potentially deadly virus that infects warm-blooded mammals.	A bacterium, which is often carried by rodents, that enters through mucous membranes and spreads quickly throughout the body.	1st stage: dog exhibits change in behavior, fear. 2nd stage: dog's behavior becomes more aggressive. 3rd stage: loss of coordination, trouble with bodily functions.
Parvovirus	Highly contagious virus, potentially deadly.	Ingestion of the virus, which is usually spread through the feces of infected dogs.	Most common: severe diarrhea. Also vomiting, fatigue, lack of appetite.
Kennel cough	Contagious respiratory infection.	Combination of types of bacteria and virus. Most common: *Bordetella bronchiseptica* bacteria and parainfluenza virus.	Chronic cough.
Distemper	Disease primarily affecting respiratory and nervous system.	Virus that is related to the human measles virus.	Mild symptoms such as fever, lack of appetite and mucus secretion progress to evidence of brain damage, "hard pad."
Hepatitis	Virus primarily affecting the liver.	Canine adenovirus type I (CAV-1). Enters system when dog breathes in particles.	Lesser symptoms include listlessness, diarrhea, vomiting. More severe symptoms include "blue-eye" (clumps of virus in eye).
Coronavirus	Virus resulting in digestive problems.	Virus is spread through infected dog's feces.	Stomach upset evidenced by lack of appetite, vomiting, diarrhea.

PARASITE BITES

Many of us are allergic to mosquito bites. The bites itch, erupt and may even become infected. Dogs have the same reaction to fleas, ticks and/or mites. When you feel the prick of the mosquito when it bites you, you have a chance to kill it with your hand. Unfortunately, when your dog is bitten by a flea, tick or mite, it can only scratch it away or bite it. By the time the dog has been bitten, the parasite has done some of its damage. It may also have laid eggs to cause further problems in the near future. The itching from parasite bites is probably due to the saliva injected into the site when the parasite sucks the dog's blood.

AIRBORNE ALLERGIES

Just as humans have hay fever, rose fever and other fevers from which they suffer during the pollinating season, many dogs suffer from the same allergies. So when the pollen count is high, your dog might suffer. However, don't expect him to sneeze and have a runny nose as a human would. Dogs react to pollen allergies the same way they react to fleas—they scratch and bite themselves. Yorkshire Terriers are very susceptible to airborne pollen allergies. Dogs, like humans, can be tested for allergens. Discuss the testing with your veterinary dermatologist.

FOOD ALLERGIES

Dogs are allergic to many foods that may be best-sellers and highly recommended by breeders and veterinarians. Changing the brand of food that you buy may not eliminate the problem because the element of the food to which the dog is allergic may also be contained in the new brand.

Recognizing a food allergy is difficult. Humans vomit or have rashes when they eat a food to which they are allergic. Dogs neither vomit nor (usually) develop a rash. Instead they itch, scratch and bite, thus making the

VACCINE ALLERGIES

Vaccines do not work all the time. Sometimes dogs are allergic to them and many times the antibodies, which are supposed to be stimulated by the vaccine, just are not produced. You should keep your dog in the veterinary clinic for an hour after he is vaccinated to be sure there are no allergic reactions.

PROPER DIET

Feeding your dog properly is very important. An incorrect diet could affect the dog's health, behavior and nervous system, possibly making a normal dog into an aggressive one. Its most visible effects are to the skin and coat, but internal organs are similarly affected.

Never neglect your Yorkie's routine check-ups and veterinary care.

diagnosis extremely difficult. While pollen allergies and parasite bites are usually seasonal, food allergies are year-round problems.

TREATING FOOD PROBLEMS

Handling food allergies and food intolerance yourself is possible. Put your dog on a diet that he has never had. Obviously if he has never eaten this new food, he can't yet have been allergic or intolerant of it. Start with a single ingredient that is *not* in the dog's diet at the present time. Ingredients like chopped beef or chicken are common in dog's diets, so try something more exotic like fish, rabbit, pheasant or some other source of quality

protein. Keep the dog on this diet (with no additives) for a month. If the symptoms of food allergy or intolerance disappear, chances are that you have defined the cause.

Don't think that the single ingredient cured the problem. You still must find a suitable diet and ascertain which ingredient in the old diet was objectionable. This is most easily done by adding ingredients to the new diet one at a time until the problem is solved. Let the dog stay on the modified diet for a month before you add another ingredient.

An alternative method is to carefully study the ingredients in the diet to which your dog is allergic or intolerant. Identify the main ingredient in this diet and eliminate the main ingredient by buying a different food which does not have that ingredient. Keep experimenting until the symptoms disappear after one month on the new diet.

Whether you have a puppy or an older dog, your children must be trained in the care and handling of a Yorkie. Yorkies are small, sensitive and dependent upon their human companions.

A male dog flea, Ctenocephalides canis.

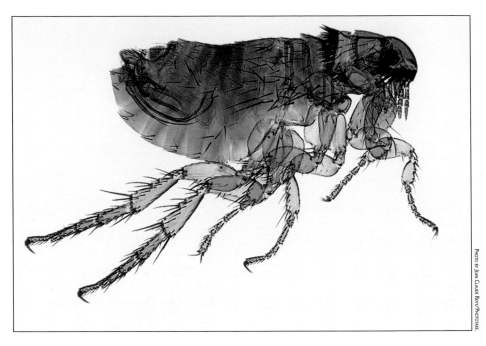

PHOTO BY JEAN CLAUDE REVY/PHOTOTAKE.

EXTERNAL PARASITES

FLEAS

Of all the problems to which dogs are prone, none is more well known and frustrating than fleas. Flea infestation is relatively simple to cure but difficult to prevent. Parasites that are harbored inside the body are a bit more difficult to eradicate but they are easier to control.

To control flea infestation, you have to understand the flea's life cycle. Fleas are often thought of as a summertime problem, but centrally heated homes have changed the patterns and fleas can be found at any time of the year. The most effective method of flea control is a two-stage approach: one stage to kill the adult fleas, and the other to control the development of pre-adult fleas. Unfortunately, no single active ingredient is effective against all stages of the life cycle.

FLEA KILLER CAUTION— "POISON"

Flea-killers are poisonous. You should not spray these toxic chemicals on areas of a dog's body that he licks, including his genitals and his face. Flea killers taken internally are a better answer, but check with your vet in case internal therapy is not advised for your dog.

LIFE CYCLE STAGES

During its life, a flea will pass through four life stages: egg, larva, pupa or nymph and adult. The adult stage is the most visible and irritating stage of the flea life cycle, and this is why the majority of flea-control products concentrate on this stage. The fact is that adult fleas account for only 1% of the total flea population, and the other 99% exist in pre-adult stages, i.e., eggs, larvae and nymphs. The pre-adult stages are barely visible to the naked eye.

THE LIFE CYCLE OF THE FLEA

Eggs are laid on the dog, usually in quantities of about 20 or 30, several times a day. The adult female flea must have a blood meal before each egg-laying session. When first laid, the eggs will cling to the dog's hair, as the eggs are still moist. However, they will quickly dry out and fall from the dog, especially if the dog moves around or scratches. Many eggs will fall off in the dog's favorite area or an area in which he spends a lot of time, such as his bed.

Once the eggs fall from the dog onto the carpet or furniture, they will hatch into larvae. This takes from one to ten days. Larvae are not particularly mobile and will usually travel only a few inches from where they hatch. However, they do have a tendency to move away from bright light and heavy

EN GARDE: CATCHING FLEAS OFF GUARD!
Consider the following ways to arm yourself against fleas:
- Add a small amount of pennyroyal or eucalyptus oil to your dog's bath. These natural remedies repel fleas.
- Supplement your dog's food with fresh garlic (minced or grated) and a hearty amount of brewer's yeast, both of which ward off fleas.
- Use a flea comb on your dog daily. Submerge fleas in a cup of bleach to kill them quickly.
- Confine the dog to only a few rooms to limit the spread of fleas in the home.
- Vacuum daily...and get all of the crevices! Dispose of the bag every few days until the problem is under control.
- Wash your dog's bedding daily. Cover cushions where your dog sleeps with towels, and wash the towels often.

traffic—under furniture and behind doors are common places to find high quantities of flea larvae.

The flea larvae feed on dead organic matter, including adult flea feces, until they are ready to change into adult fleas. Fleas will usually remain as larvae for around seven days. After this period, the larvae will pupate into protective pupae. While inside the pupae, the larvae will undergo

metamorphosis and change into
adult fleas. This can take as little
time as a few days, but the adult
fleas can remain inside the pupae
waiting to hatch for up to two
years. The pupae are signaled to
hatch by certain stimuli, such as
physical pressure—the pupae's
being stepped on, heat from an
animal's lying on the pupae or
increased carbon-dioxide levels
and vibrations—indicating that a
suitable host is available.

Once hatched, the adult flea
must feed within a few days.
Once the adult flea finds a host, it
will not leave voluntarily. It only
becomes dislodged by grooming
or the host animal's scratching.

The adult flea will remain on the
host for the duration of its life
unless forcibly removed.

TREATING THE ENVIRONMENT
AND THE DOG

Treating fleas should be a two-
pronged attack. First, the
environment needs to be treated;
this includes carpets and
furniture, especially the dog's
bedding and areas underneath
furniture. The environment
should be treated with a
household spray containing an
Insect Growth Regulator (IGR) and
an insecticide to kill the adult
fleas. Most IGRs are effective
against eggs and larvae; they
actually mimic the fleas' own
hormones and stop the eggs and
larvae from developing into adult
fleas. There are currently no
treatments available to attack the
pupa stage of the life cycle, so the
adult insecticide is used to kill
the newly hatched adult fleas
before they find a host. Most IGRs
are active for many months, while

A scanning
electron
micrograph of a
dog or cat flea,
Ctenocephalides,
magnified more
than 100x.
This image has
been colorized
for effect.

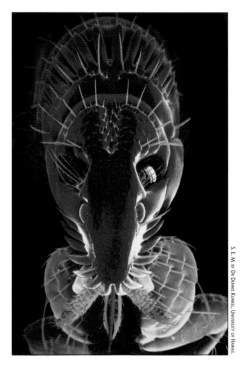

THE LIFE CYCLE OF THE FLEA

Adult

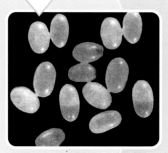

Egg

Pupa or Nymph

PHOTOS COURTESY OF FLEABUSTERS® RX FOR FLEAS.

Larva

A LOOK AT FLEAS

Fleas have been around for millions of years and have adapted to changing host animals. They are able to go through a complete life cycle in less than one month or they can extend their lives to almost two years by remaining as pupae or cocoons. They do not need blood or any other food for up to 20 months.

INSECT GROWTH REGULATOR (IGR)

Two types of products should be used when treating fleas—a product to treat the pet and a product to treat the home. Adult fleas represent less than 1% of the flea population. The pre-adult fleas (eggs, larvae and pupae) represent more than 99% of the flea population and are found in the environment; it is in the case of pre-adult fleas that products containing an Insect Growth Regulator (IGR) should be used in the home.

IGRs are a new class of compounds used to prevent the development of insects. They do not kill the insect outright, but instead use the insect's biology against it to stop it from completing its growth. Products that contain methoprene are the world's first and leading IGRs. Used to control fleas and other insects, this type of IGR will stop flea larvae from developing and protect the house for up to seven months.

The American dog tick, *Dermacentor variabilis*, is probably the most common tick found on dogs. Look at the strength in its eight legs! No wonder it's hard to detach them.

adult insecticides are only active for a few days.

When treating with a household spray, it is a good idea to vacuum before applying the product. This stimulates as many pupae as possible to hatch into adult fleas. The vacuum cleaner should also be treated with an insecticide to prevent the eggs and larvae that have been collected in the vacuum bag from hatching.

The second stage of treatment is to apply an adult insecticide to the dog. Traditionally, this would be in the form of a collar or a spray, but more recent innovations include digestible insecticides that poison the fleas when they ingest the dog's blood. Alternatively, there are drops that, when placed on the back of the dog's neck, spread throughout the hair and skin to kill adult fleas.

TICKS

Though not as common as fleas, ticks are found all over the tropical and temperate world. They don't bite, like fleas; they harpoon. They dig their sharp proboscis (nose) into the dog's skin and drink the blood. Their

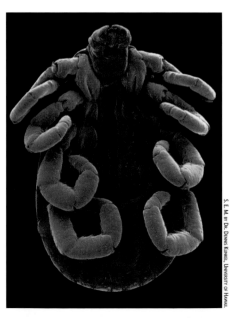

S. E. M. BY DR. DENNIS KUNKEL, UNIVERSITY OF HAWAII

only food and drink is dog's blood. Dogs can get Lyme disease, Rocky Mountain spotted fever, tick bite paralysis and many other diseases from ticks. They may live where fleas are found and they like to hide in cracks or seams in walls. They are controlled the same way fleas are controlled.

The American dog tick, *Dermacentor variabilis*, may well be the most common dog tick in many geographical areas, especially those areas where the climate is hot and humid. Most dog ticks have life expectancies of a week to six months, depending upon climatic conditions. They can neither jump nor fly, but they can crawl slowly and can range up to 16 feet to reach a sleeping or unsuspecting dog.

MITES

Just as fleas and ticks can be problematic for your dog, mites can also lead to an itchy nuisance. Microscopic in size, mites are related to ticks and generally take up permanent residence on their host animal— in this case, your dog! The term *mange* refers to any infestation caused by one of the mighty mites, of which there are six varieties that concern dog owners.

Demodex mites cause a condition known as demodicosis

DEER-TICK CROSSING

The great outdoors may be fun for your dog, but it also is a home to dangerous ticks. Deer ticks carry a bacterium known as *Borrelia burgdorferi* and are most active in the autumn and spring. When infections are caught early, penicillin and tetracycline are effective antibiotics, but, if left untreated, the bacteria may cause neurological, kidney and cardiac problems as well as long-term trouble with walking and painful joints.

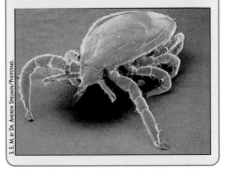

S. E. M. BY DR. ANDREW SPIELMAN/PHOTOTAKE.

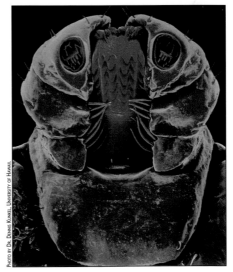

PHOTO BY DR. DENNIS KUNKEL, UNIVERSITY OF HAWAII.

The head of an American dog tick, *Dermacentor variabilis*, enlarged and colorized for effect.

PHOTO BY JAMES HAYDEN/YOAV/PHOTOTAKE.

(sometimes called red mange or follicular mange), in which the mites live in larger than normal numbers in the dog's hair follicles and sebaceous glands. This type of mange is commonly passed from the dam to her puppies and usually shows up on the puppies' muzzles, though demodicosis is not transferable from one normal dog to another. Most dogs recover from this type of mange without any treatment, though topical therapies are commonly prescribed by the vet.

Human lice look like dog lice; the two are closely related.
PHOTO BY DWIGHT R. KUHN.

The *Cheyletiellosis* mite is the hook-mouthed culprit associated with "walking dandruff," a condition that affects dogs as well as cats and rabbits. This mite lives on the surface of the animal's skin and is readily transferable through direct or indirect contact with an affected animal. The dandruff is present in the form of scaly skin, which may or may not be itchy. If not treated, this mange can affect a whole kennel of dogs and can be spread to humans as well.

The *Sarcoptes* mite causes intense itching on the dog in the form of a condition known as scabies or sarcoptic mange. The cycle of the *Sarcoptes* mite lasts about three weeks, and the mites live in the top layer of the dog's skin (epidermis), preferably in areas with little hair. Scabies is highly contagious and can be passed to humans. Sometimes an allergic reaction to the mite worsens the severe itching associated with sarcoptic mange.

Ear mites, *Otodectes cynotis,* lead to otodectic mange, which most commonly affects the outer ear canal of the dog, though other areas can be affected as well. Dogs with ear-mite infestation commonly scratch at their ears, causing further irritation, and shake their heads. Dark brown droppings in the outer ear confirm the diagnosis. Your vet can prescribe a treatment to flush out the ears and kill any eggs in the ears. A complete month of treatment is necessary to cure the mange.

Two other mites, less common in dogs, include *Dermanyssus gallinae* (the poultry or red mite) and *Eutrombicula alfreddugesi* (the North American mite associated with trombiculidiasis or chigger infestation). The poultry mite frequently lives on chickens, but can transfer to dogs who spend time near farm animals. Chigger infestation affects dogs in the

---

NOT A DROP TO DRINK

Never allow your dog to swim in polluted water or public areas where water quality can be suspect. Even perfectly clear water can harbor parasites, many of which can cause serious to fatal illnesses in canines. Areas inhabited by water-fowl and other wildlife are especially dangerous.

Central U.S. who have exposure to woodlands. The types of mange caused by both of these mites are treatable by veterinarians.

INTERNAL PARASITES

Most animals—fishes, birds and mammals, including dogs and humans—have worms and other parasites that live inside their bodies. According to Dr. Herbert R. Axelrod, the fish pathologist, there are two kinds of parasites: dumb and smart. The smart parasites live in peaceful cooperation with their hosts (symbiosis), while the dumb parasites kill their hosts. Most worm infections are relatively easy to control. If they are not controlled, they weaken the host dog to the point that other medical problems occur, but they do not kill the host as dumb parasites would.

A brown dog tick, *Rhipicephalus sanguineus*, is an uncommon but annoying tick found on dogs.

DO NOT MIX

Never mix parasite-control products without first consulting your vet. Some products can become toxic when combined with others and can cause fatal consequences.

The roundworm *Rhabditis* can infect both dogs and humans.

The roundworm, *Ascaris lumbricoides.*

ROUNDWORMS

Average-size dogs can pass 1,360,000 roundworm eggs every day. For example, if there were only 1 million dogs in the world, the world would be saturated with thousands of tons of dog feces. These feces would contain around 15,000,000,000 roundworm eggs.

Up to 31% of home yards and children's sand boxes in the US contain roundworm eggs.

Flushing dog's feces down the toilet is not a safe practice because the usual sewage treatments do not destroy roundworm eggs.

Infected puppies start shedding roundworm eggs at three weeks of age. They can be infected by their mother's milk.

ROUNDWORMS

The roundworms that infect dogs are known scientifically as *Toxocara canis.* They live in the dog's intestines and shed eggs continually. It has been estimated that a dog produces about 6 or more ounces of feces every day. Each ounce of feces averages hundreds of thousands of roundworm eggs. There are no known areas in which dogs roam that do not contain roundworm eggs. The greatest danger of roundworms is that they infect people, too! It is wise to have your dog tested regularly for roundworms.

In young puppies, roundworms cause bloated bellies, diarrhea, coughing and vomiting, and are transmitted from the dam (through blood or milk). Affected puppies will not appear as animated as normal puppies. The worms appear spaghetti-like, measuring as long as 6 inches. Adult dogs can acquire roundworms through coprophagia (eating contaminated feces) or by killing rodents that carry roundworms.

Roundworm infection can kill puppies and cause severe problems in adults, as the hatched larvae travel to the lungs and trachea through the bloodstream. Cleanliness is the best preventative for roundworms. Always pick up after your dog and dispose of feces in appropriate receptacles.

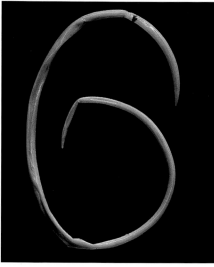

PHOTO BY DWIGHT R. KUHN.

HOOKWORMS

In the United States, dog owners have to be concerned about four different species of hookworm, the most common and most serious of which is *Ancylostoma caninum,* which prefers warm climates. The others are *Ancylostoma braziliense, Ancylostoma tubaeforme* and *Uncinaria stenocephala,* the latter of which is a concern to dogs living in the Northern U.S. and Canada, as this species prefers cold climates. Hookworms are dangerous to humans as well as to dogs and cats, and can be the cause of severe anemia due to iron deficiency. The worm uses its teeth to attach itself to the dog's intestines and changes the site of its attachment about six times per day. Each time the worm repositions itself, the dog loses

blood and can become anemic. *Ancylostoma caninum* is the most likely of the four species to cause anemia in the dog.

Symptoms of hookworm infection include dark stools, weight loss, general weakness, pale coloration and anemia, as well as possible skin problems. Fortunately, hookworms are easily purged from the affected dog with a number of medications that have proven effective. Discuss these with your veterinarian. Most heartworm preventatives include a hookworm insecticide as well.

Owners also must be aware that hookworms can infect humans, who can acquire the larvae through exposure to contaminated feces. Since the worms cannot complete their life cycle on a human, the worms simply infest the skin and cause irritation. This condition is known as cutaneous larva migrans syndrome. As a preventative, use disposable gloves or a "poop-scoop" to pick up your dog's droppings and prevent your dog (or neighborhood cats) from defecating in children's play areas.

The hookworm, *Ancylostoma caninum.*

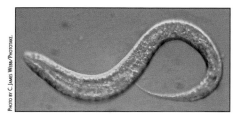

PHOTO BY C. JAMES WEBB/PHOTOTAKE.

The infective stage of the hookworm larva.

TAPEWORMS

Humans, rats, squirrels, foxes, coyotes, wolves and domestic dogs are all susceptible to tapeworm infection. Except in humans, tapeworms are usually not a fatal infection. Infected individuals can harbor 1000 parasitic worms.

Tapeworms, like some other types of worm, are hermaphroditic, meaning male and female in the same worm.

If dogs eat infected rats or mice, or anything else infected with tapeworm, they get the tapeworm disease. One month after attaching to a dog's intestine, the worm starts shedding eggs. These eggs are infective immediately. Infective eggs can live for a few months without a host animal.

The head and rostellum (the round prominence on the scolex) of a tapeworm, which infects dogs and humans.

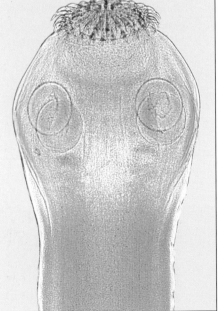

PHOTO BY CAROLINA BIOLOGICAL SUPPLY/PHOTOTAKE.

TAPEWORMS

There are many species of tapeworm, all of which are carried by fleas! The most common tapeworm affecting dogs is known as *Dipylidium caninum*. The dog eats the flea and starts the tapeworm cycle. Humans can also be infected with tapeworms—so don't eat fleas! Fleas are so small that your dog could pass them onto your hands, your plate or your food and thus make it possible for you to ingest a flea that is carrying tapeworm eggs.

While tapeworm infection is not life-threatening in dogs (smart parasite!), it can be the cause of a very serious liver disease for humans. About 50% of the humans infected with *Echinococcus multilocularis*, a type of tapeworm that causes alveolar hydatid, perish.

WHIPWORMS

In North America, whipworms are counted among the most common parasitic worms in dogs. The whipworm's scientific name is *Trichuris vulpis*. These worms attach themselves in the lower parts of the intestine, where they feed. Affected dogs may only experience upset tummies, colic and diarrhea. These worms, however, can live for months or years in the dog, beginning their larval stage in the small intestine, spending their adult stage in the large intestine and finally passing infective eggs through the dog's feces. The only way to detect whipworms is through a fecal examination, though this is not always foolproof. Treatment for whipworms is tricky, due to the worms' unusual life-cycle pattern, and very often dogs are reinfected due to exposure to infective eggs on the ground. The whipworm eggs can survive in the environment for as long as five years, thus cleaning up droppings in your own backyard as well as in public places is absolutely essential for sanitation purposes and the health of your dog and others.

THREADWORMS

Though less common than roundworms, hookworms and those mentioned previously, threadworms concern dog owners in the Southwestern U.S. and Gulf Coast area where the climate is hot and humid. Living in the small intestine of the dog, this worm measures a mere 2 millimeters and is round in shape. Like that of the whipworm, the threadworm's life cycle is very complex and the eggs and larvae are passed through the feces. A deadly disease in humans, *Strongyloides* readily infects people, and the handling of feces is the most common means of transmission. Threadworms are most often seen in young puppies; bloody diarrhea and pneumonia are symptoms. Sick puppies must be isolated and treated immediately; vets recommend a follow-up treatment one month later.

HEARTWORM PREVENTATIVES

There are many heartworm preventatives on the market, many of which are sold at your veterinarian's office. These products can be given daily or monthly, depending on the manufacturer's instructions. All of these preventatives contain chemical insecticides directed at killing heartworms, which leads to some controversy among dog owners. In effect, heartworm preventatives are necessary evils, though you should determine how necessary based on your pet's lifestyle. There is no doubt that heartworm is a dreadful disease that threatens the lives of dogs. However, the likelihood of your dog's being bitten by an infected mosquito is slim in most places, and a mosquito-repellent (or an herbal remedy such as Wormwood or Black Walnut) is much safer for your dog and will not compromise his immune system (the way heartworm preventatives will). Should you decide to use the traditional preventative "medications," you can consider giving the pill every other or third month. Since the toxins in the pill will kill the heartworms at all stages of development, the pill would be effective in killing larvae, nymphs or adults and it takes four months for the larvae to reach the adult stage. Thus, there is no rationale to poisoning the dog's system on a monthly basis. Lastly, do not give the pill during the winter months since there are no mosquitoes around to pass on their infection, unless you live in a tropical environment.

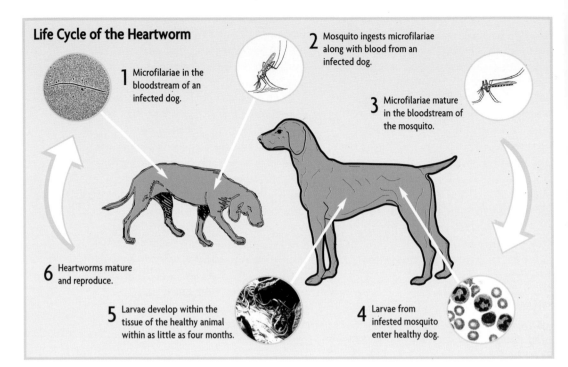

Life Cycle of the Heartworm

1 Microfilariae in the bloodstream of an infected dog.

2 Mosquito ingests microfilariae along with blood from an infected dog.

3 Microfilariae mature in the bloodstream of the mosquito.

6 Heartworms mature and reproduce.

5 Larvae develop within the tissue of the healthy animal within as little as four months.

4 Larvae from infested mosquito enter healthy dog.

HEARTWORMS

Heartworms are thin, extended worms up to 12 inches long, which live in a dog's heart and the major blood vessels surrounding it. Dogs may have up to 200 worms. Symptoms may be loss of energy, loss of appetite, coughing, the development of a pot belly and anemia.

Heartworms are transmitted by mosquitoes. The mosquito drinks the blood of an infected dog and takes in larvae with the blood. The larvae, called microfilariae, develop within the body of the mosquito and are passed on to the next dog bitten after the larvae mature. It takes two to three weeks for the larvae to develop to the infective stage within the body of the mosquito. Dogs are usually treated at about six weeks of age and maintained on a prophylactic dose given monthly.

Blood testing for heartworms is not necessarily indicative of how seriously your dog is infected. Although this is a dangerous disease, it is not easy for a dog to be infected. Discuss the various preventatives with your vet, as there are many different types now available. Together you can decide on a safe course of prevention for your dog.

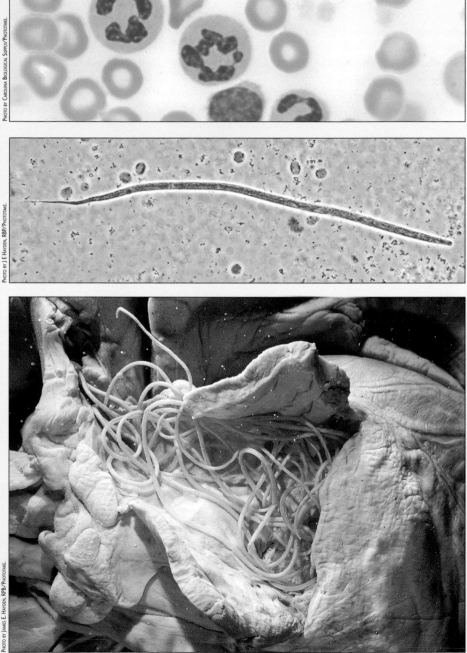

PHOTO BY CAROLINA BIOLOGICAL SUPPLY/PHOTOTAKE.

Magnified heartworm larvae, *Dirofilaria immitis.*

PHOTO BY J E HAYDEN, RBP/PHOTOTAKE.

Heartworm, *Dirofilaria immitis.*

PHOTO BY JAMES E. HAYDEN, RPB/PHOTOTAKE.

The heart of a dog infected with canine heartworm, *Dirofilaria immitis.*

Number-One Killer Disease in Dogs: CANCER

In every age, there is a word associated with a disease or plague that causes humans to shudder. In the 21st century, that word is "cancer." Just as cancer is the leading cause of death in humans, it claims nearly half the lives of dogs that die from a natural disease as well as half the dogs that die over the age of ten years.

Described as a genetic disease, cancer becomes a greater risk as the dog ages. Veterinarians and dog owners have become increasingly aware of the threat of cancer to dogs. Statistics reveal that one dog in every five will develop cancer, the most common of which is skin cancer. Many cancers, including prostate, ovarian and breast cancer, can be avoided by spaying and neutering our dogs by the age of six months.

Early detection of cancer can save or extend your dog's life, so it is absolutely vital for owners to have their dogs examined by a qualified veterinarian or oncologist immediately upon detection of any abnormality. Certain dietary guidelines have also proven to reduce the onset and spread of cancer. Foods based on fish rather than beef, due to the presence of Omega-3 fatty acids, are recommended. Other amino acids such as glutamine have significant benefits for canines, particularly those breeds that show a greater susceptibility to cancer.

Cancer management and treatments promise hope for future generations of canines. Since the disease is genetic, breeders should never breed a dog whose parents, grandparents and any related siblings have developed cancer. It is difficult to know whether to exclude an otherwise healthy dog from a breeding program as the disease does not manifest itself until the dog's senior years.

RECOGNIZE CANCER WARNING SIGNS

Since early detection can possibly rescue your dog from becoming a cancer statistic, it is essential for owners to recognize the possible signs and seek the assistance of a qualified professional.

- Abnormal bumps or lumps that continue to grow
- Bleeding or discharge from any body cavity
- Persistent stiffness or lameness
- Recurrent sores or sores that do not heal
- Inappetence
- Breathing difficulties
- Weight loss
- Bad breath or odors
- General malaise and fatigue
- Eating and swallowing problems
- Difficulty urinating and defecating

Disease	Percentage
Cancer	47%
Heart disease	12%
Kidney disease	7%
Epilepsy	4%
Liver disease	4%
Bloat	3%
Diabetes	3%
Stroke	2%
Cushing's disease	2%
Immune diseases	2%
Other causes	14%

The Ten Most Common Fatal Diseases in Pure-bred Dogs

Your Senior Yorkshire Terrier

The term *old* is a qualitative term. For dogs, as well as their masters, old is relative. Certainly we can all distinguish between a puppy Yorkshire Terrier and an adult Yorkshire Terrier—there are the obvious physical traits such as size and appearance, and personality traits like their antics and the expressions on their faces. Puppies and young dogs like to play with children. Children's natural exuberance is a good match for the seemingly endless energy of young dogs. They like to run, jump, chase and retrieve. When dogs grow up and cease their interaction with children, they are often thought of as being too old to play with the kids.

On the other hand, if a Yorkshire Terrier is only exposed to people with quieter lifestyles, his life will normally be less active and the decrease in his activity level as he ages will not be as obvious.

If people live to be 100 years

As your Yorkie gets older, physical and behavioral problems and changes occur. Always treat your senior with respect and special care.

When your Yorkie stops retrieving or loses interest in physical activities, you should refrain from initiating such activities too regularly.

old, dogs live to be 20 years old. While this is a good rule of thumb, it is *very* inaccurate. When trying to compare dog years to human years, you cannot make a generalization about all dogs. You can make the generalization that 14 years is a good lifespan for a Yorkshire Terrier. Dogs are generally considered mature within three years, but they can reproduce even earlier. So the first three years of a dog's life are more like seven times that of comparable humans. That means a

3-year-old dog is like a 21-year-old person. As the curve of comparison shows, there is no hard and fast rule for comparing dog and human ages. The comparison is made even more difficult, for not all humans age at the same rate...and human females live longer than human males.

WHAT TO LOOK FOR IN SENIORS

Most vets and behaviorists use the seven-year-old mark as the time to consider a dog a senior, though some breeders prefer to wait until the Yorkshire Terrier is eight or nine years of age. Nevertheless, the term *senior* does not imply that the dog is geriatric and has begun to fail in mind and body. Aging is essentially a slowing process. Humans readily admit that they feel a difference in their activity level from age 20 to 30, and then from 30 to 40, etc. By treating the

NOTICING THE SYMPTOMS

The symptoms listed below are symptoms that gradually appear and become more noticeable. They are not life-threatening; however, the symptoms below are to be taken very seriously and warrant a discussion with your veterinarian:

• Your dog cries and whimpers when he moves, and he stops running completely.

• Convulsions start or become more serious and frequent. The usual convulsion (spasm) is when the dog stiffens and starts to tremble, being unable or unwilling to move. The seizure usually lasts for 5 to 30 minutes.

• Your dog drinks more water and urinates more frequently. Wetting and bowel accidents take place indoors without warning.

• Vomiting becomes more and more frequent.

seven-year-old dog as a senior, owners are able to implement certain therapeutic and preventative medical strategies with the help of their veterinarians. A senior-care program should include at least two veterinary visits per year and screening sessions to determine the dog's health status, as well as nutritional counseling. Vets determine the senior dog's health status through a blood smear for a complete blood count, serum chemistry profile with electrolytes, urinalysis, blood pressure check, electrocardiogram, ocular tonometry (pressure on the eyeball) and dental prophylaxis.

Such an extensive program for senior dogs is well advised before owners start to see the obvious physical signs of aging, such as slower and inhibited movement, graying, increased sleep/nap periods and disinterest in play and other activity. This preventative program promises a longer, healthier life for the aging dog. Among the physical problems common in aging dogs are the loss of sight and hearing, arthritis, kidney and liver failure, diabetes mellitus, heart disease and Cushing's disease (a hormonal disease).

In addition to the physical manifestations discussed, there are some behavioral changes and problems related to aging dogs. Dogs

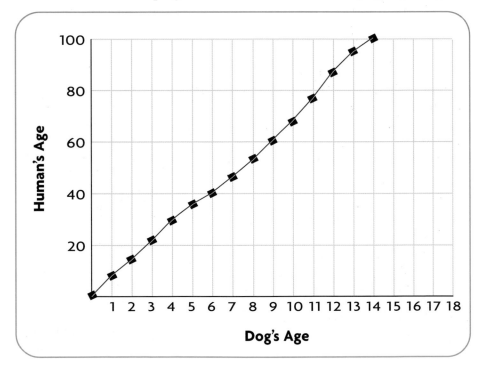

suffering from hearing or vision loss, dental discomfort or arthritis can become aggressive. Likewise, the near-deaf and/or blind dog may be startled more easily and react in an unexpectedly aggressive manner. Seniors suffering from senility can become more impatient and irritable. Housesoiling accidents are associated with loss of mobility, kidney problems and loss of sphincter control as well as plaque accumulation, physiological brain changes and reactions to medications. Older dogs, just like young puppies, suffer from separation anxiety, which can lead to excessive barking, whining, housesoiling and destructive behavior. Seniors may become fearful of everyday sounds, such as vacuum cleaners, heaters, thunder and passing traffic. Some dogs have diffi-

culty sleeping, due to discomfort, the need for frequent potty visits and the like.

Owners should avoid spoiling the older dog with too many fatty treats. Obesity is a common problem in older dogs and subtracts years from their lives. Keep the senior dog as trim as possible, since excessive weight puts additional stress on the body's vital organs. Some breeders recommend supplementing the diet with foods high in fiber and lower in calories. Adding fresh vegetables and marrow broth to the senior's diet makes a tasty, low-calorie, low-fat supplement. Vets also offer specialty diets for senior dogs that are worth exploring.

Your dog, as he nears his twilight years, needs your patience and good care more than

Consult your vet to help you locate a pet cemetery in your area.

ever. Never punish an older dog for an accident or abnormal behavior. For all the years of love, protection and companionship that your dog has provided, he deserves special attention and courtesies. The older dog may need to relieve himself at 3 a.m. because he can no longer hold it for eight hours. Older dogs may not be able to remain crated for more than two or three hours. Although he may not seem as enthusiastic about your attention and petting, he does appreciate the considerations you offer as he gets older.

Your Yorkshire Terrier does not understand why his world is slowing down. Owners must make their dogs' transition into their golden years as pleasant and rewarding as possible.

WHAT TO DO WHEN THE TIME COMES

You are never fully prepared to make a rational decision about putting your dog to sleep. It is very obvious that you love your Yorkshire Terrier or you would not be reading this book. Putting a beloved dog to sleep is extremely difficult. It is a decision that must be made with your vet. You are usually forced to make the decision when your dog experiences one or more life-threatening symptoms that have become serious enough for you to seek veterinary help. If the prognosis of the malady indicates that the end is near and that your beloved pet will only continue to suffer and experience no enjoyment for the balance of his life, then euthanasia is the right choice.

WHAT IS EUTHANASIA?

Euthanasia derives from the Greek, meaning *good death*. In other words, it means the planned, painless killing of a dog suffering from a painful, incurable condition, or who is so aged that he cannot walk, see, eat or control his excretory functions. Euthanasia is usually accomplished by injection with an overdose of anesthesia or a barbiturate. Aside from the prick of the needle, the experience is usually painless.

MAKING THE DECISION

The decision to euthanize your dog is never easy. The days during which the dog becomes ill and the end occurs can be unusually stressful for you. If this is your first experience with the death of a loved one, you may need the comfort dictated by your religious beliefs. If you are the head of the family and have children, you should have involved them in the decision of putting your Yorkshire Terrier to sleep. Usually your dog can be maintained on drugs for a few days in order to give you ample time to make a decision. During this time, talking with members of your family or with people who have lived through the same experience can ease the burden of your inevitable decision.

THE FINAL RESTING PLACE

Dogs can have some of the same privileges as humans. The remains of your beloved dog can be buried in a pet cemetery, which is generally expensive. Dogs who have died at home can be buried on your property in a place suitably marked with some stone or newly planted tree or bush. Alternatively, your dog can be cremated individually and the ashes returned to you. A less expensive option is mass cremation, although, of course, the ashes cannot then be returned. Vets can usually arrange the cremation on your behalf. The cost of these options should always be discussed frankly and openly with your vet.

GETTING ANOTHER DOG?

The grief of losing your beloved dog will be as lasting as the grief of losing a human friend or relative. In most cases, if your dog died of old age (if there is such a thing), he had slowed down considerably. Do you want a new Yorkshire Terrier puppy to replace him? Or are you better off finding a more mature Yorkshire Terrier, say two to three years of age, which will usually be house-trained and will have an already developed personality. In this case, you can find out if you like each other after a few hours of being together.

The decision is, of course, your own. Do you want another Yorkshire Terrier or perhaps a different breed so as to avoid comparison with your beloved friend? Most people usually buy the same breed because they know (and love) the characteristics of that breed. Then, too, they often know people who have the same breed and perhaps they are lucky enough that one of their friends expects a litter soon. What could be better?

Grave stones or other types of markers are common in pet cemeteries.

CDS: COGNITIVE DYSFUNCTION SYNDROME
"Old-Dog Syndrome"

There are many ways to evaluate old-dog syndrome. Veterinarians have defined CDS (cognitive dysfunction syndrome) as the gradual deterioration of cognitive abilities. These are indicated by changes in the dog's behavior. When a dog changes its routine response, and maladies have been eliminated as the cause of these behavioral changes, then CDS is the usual diagnosis.

More than half the dogs over 8 years old suffer some form of CDS. The older the dog, the more chance it has of suffering from CDS. In humans, doctors often dismiss the CDS behavioral changes as part of "winding down."

There are four major signs of CDS: exhibits frequent bathroom accidents inside the home, sleeping much more or much less than normal, acting confused and failing to respond to social stimuli.

SYMPTOMS OF CDS

FREQUENT POTTY ACCIDENTS
- *Urinates in the house.*
- *Defecates in the house.*
- *Doesn't signal that he wants to go out.*

SLEEP PATTERNS
- *Moves much more slowly.*
- *Sleeps more than normal during the day.*
- *Sleeps less during the night.*

CONFUSION
- *Goes outside and just stands there.*
- *Appears confused with a faraway look in his eyes.*
- *Hides more often.*
- *Doesn't recognize friends.*
- *Doesn't come when called.*
- *Walks around listlessly and without a destination goal.*

FAILURE TO RESPOND TO SOCIAL STIMULI
- *Comes to people less frequently, whether called or not.*
- *Doesn't tolerate petting for more than a short time.*
- *Doesn't come to the door when you return home from work.*

Your show Yorkie loves to be dressed up for the big event. Grooming is a major effort in dog show participation as Yorkies must be carefully groomed for showing and it takes effort on your part to learn how to groom and maintain the coat on a daily basis.

Showing Your Yorkshire Terrier

When you purchase your Yorkshire Terrier, you will make it clear to the breeder whether you want one just as a lovable companion and pet, or if you hope to be buying a Yorkshire Terrier with show prospects. No reputable breeder will sell you a young puppy and tell you that he is *definitely* of show quality, for so much can go wrong during the early months of a puppy's development. If you plan to show, what you will hopefully have acquired is a puppy with "show potential."

To the novice, exhibiting a Yorkshire Terrier in the show ring may look easy, but it takes a lot of hard work and devotion to do top winning at a show such as the prestigious Westminster Kennel Club dog show, not to mention a little luck too!

The way your Yorkie moves, his gait, is one of the criteria upon which the dog is judged.

AKC GROUPS
For showing purposes, the American Kennel Club divides its recognized breeds into seven groups: Toy Dogs, Sporting Dogs, Hounds, Working Dogs, Terriers, Non-Sporting Dogs and Herding Dogs.

The first concept that the canine novice learns when watching a dog show is that each dog first competes against members of his own breed. Once the judge has selected the best member of each breed (Best of Breed), provided that the show is judged on a Group system, that chosen dog will compete with

If your Yorkie is of show quality, you really should explore conformation showing through your local breed club.

the other Best of Breed dogs in his group. Finally, the dogs chosen first in each group will compete for Best in Show.

The second concept that you must understand is that the dogs are not actually compared against one another. The judge compares each dog against his respective breed standard, the approved word depiction of the ideal specimen that is approved by the American Kennel Club (AKC). While some early breed standards

The evaluation of your Yorkie by an experienced judge can be very enlightening.

were indeed based on specific dogs that were famous or popular, many dedicated enthusiasts say that a perfect specimen, as described in the standard, has never walked into a show ring, has never been bred and, to the woe of dog breeders around the globe, does not exist. Breeders attempt to get as close to this ideal as possible with every litter, but theoretically the "perfect" dog is so elusive that it is impossible. (And if the "perfect" dog were born, breeders and judges would never agree that it was indeed "perfect.")

If you are interested in exploring the world of dog showing, your best bet is to join your local breed club or the national parent club, which is the Yorkshire Terrier Club of America. These clubs often host both regional and national specialties,

This wind-blown show dog has the appearance of a well-trained contender. With dedication, patience and experience, you can show and win with your Yorkie at a conformation event.

BECOMING A CHAMPION

An official AKC champion of record requires that a dog accumulate 15 points under three different judges, including two "majors" under different judges. Points are awarded based on the number of dogs entered into competition, varying from breed to breed and place to place. A win of three, four or five points is considered a "major." The AKC annually assigns a schedule of points to adjust to the variations that accompany a breed's popularity and the population of a given area.

shows only for Yorkshire Terriers, which can include conformation as well as obedience and agility trials. Even if you have no intention of competing with your Yorkshire Terrier, a specialty is like a festival for lovers of the breed who congregate to share their favorite topic: Yorkies! Clubs also send out newsletters, and some organize training days and seminars in order that people may learn more about their chosen breed. To locate the breed club closest to you, contact the American Kennel Club (AKC), which furnishes the rules and regulations for all of these events plus general dog registration and other basic requirements of dog ownership.

In the U.S., the AKC offers three kinds of conformation shows: an all-breed show (for all AKC-recognized breeds), a

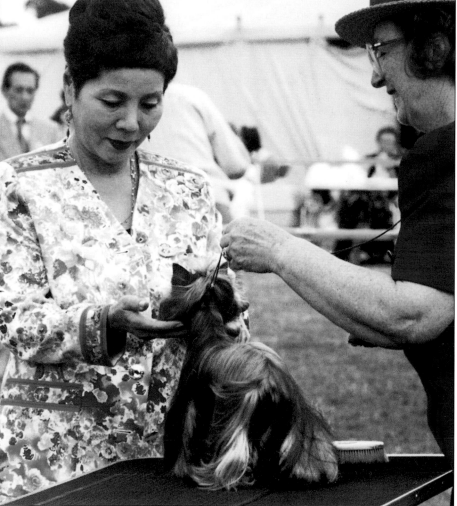

Dog shows are fun as well as educational. You can expect to meet a lot of nice people in the show dog circuit.

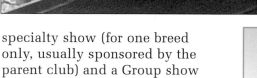

specialty show (for one breed only, usually sponsored by the parent club) and a Group show (for all breeds in the Group).

For a dog to become an AKC champion of record, the dog must accumulate 15 points at the shows from at least three differ-

COLOR CONFUSION

The first-prize winner in America collects a blue ribbon and prize card. In Britain, blue goes to the second-place winner, and it is the red rosette that is awarded to the first-place winner. This difference in colors has led to some embarrassing situations when some have judged away from home!

SHOW-RING ETIQUETTE

Just as with anything else, there is a certain etiquette to the show ring that can only be learned through experience. Showing your dog can be quite intimidating to you as a novice when it seems as if everyone else knows what he is doing. You can familiarize yourself with ring procedure beforehand by taking showing classes to prepare you and your dog for conformation showing and by talking with experienced handlers. When you are in the ring, it is very important to pay attention and listen to the instructions you are given by the judge about where to move your dog. Remember, even the most skilled handlers had to start somewhere.

ent judges, including two "majors." A "major" is defined as a three-, four- or five-point win, and the number of points per win is determined on the number of dogs entered in the show on that day. Depending on the breed, the number of points that are awarded varies. In a breed as popular as the Yorkshire Terrier, more dogs are needed to rack up the points. At any dog show, only one dog and one bitch of each breed can win points.

Dog showing does not offer "co-ed" classes. Dogs and bitches never compete against each other in the classes. Non-champion dogs are called "class dogs" because they compete in one of five classes. Dogs are entered in a particular class depending on their age and previous show wins. To begin, there is the Puppy Class (for 6- to 9-month-olds and for 9- to 12-month-olds); this class is followed by the Novice Class (for dogs that have not won any first prizes except in the Puppy Class or three first prizes in the Novice Class and have not accumulated any points toward their champion title); the Bred-by-Exhibitor Class (for dogs handled by their breeders or handled by one of the breeder's immediate family); American-bred Class (for dogs bred in the U.S.!); and the Open Class (for any dog that is not a champion).

The judge at the show begins

judging the Puppy Class, first dogs and then bitches, and proceeds through the classes. The judge places his winners first through fourth in each class. In the Winners Class, the first-place winners of each class compete with one another to determine Winners Dog and Winners Bitch. The judge also places a Reserve Winners Dog and Reserve Winners Bitch, which could be awarded the points in the case of a disqualification. The Winners Dog and Winners Bitch are the two that are awarded the points for the breed, then compete with any champions of record entered in the show. The judge reviews the Winners Dog, Winners Bitch and all of the champions to select his Best of Breed. The Best of Winners is selected between the Winners Dog and Winners Bitch. Were one of these two to be selected Best of Breed, he would automatically be named Best of

There is hardly a more pleasuresome experience for a Yorkie owner than winning at an important dog show.

Winners as well. Finally the judge selects his Best of Opposite Sex to the Best of Breed winner.

At a Group show or all-breed show, the Best of Breed winners from each breed then compete against one another for Group One through Group Four. The judge compares each Best of Breed to his breed standard, and the dog that most closely lives up to the ideal for his breed is selected as Group One. Finally, all seven group winners (from the Toy Group, Sporting Group, Hound Group, etc.) compete for Best in Show.

To find out about dog shows in your area, you can subscribe to the American Kennel Club's monthly magazine, the American Kennel Gazette and the accompanying Events Calendar. You can also look in your local newspa-

NEATNESS COUNTS

Surely you've spent hours grooming your dog to perfection for the show ring, but don't forget about yourself! While the dog should be the center of attention, it is important that you also appear neat and clean. Wear smart, appropriate clothes and comfortable shoes in a color that contrasts with your dog's coat. Look and act like a professional.

per for advertisements for dog shows in your area or go on the Internet to the AKC's website, www.akc.org.

If your Yorkshire Terrier is six months of age or older and registered with the AKC, you can enter him in a dog show where the breed is offered classes. Provided that your Yorkshire Terrier does not have a disqualifying fault, he can compete. Only unaltered dogs can be entered in a dog show, so if you have spayed or neutered your Yorkshire Terrier, you cannot compete in conformation shows. The reason for this is simple. Dog shows are the main forum to prove which representatives in a breed are worthy of being bred. Only dogs that have achieved championships—the AKC "seal of approval" for quality in pure-

Eng. Ch. Ozmilion Mystification, owned and handled by Osman Sameja, was the first Yorkshire Terrier to win Best in Show at Crufts, the most prestigious show in England.

A champion-quality Yorkie, perfectly groomed, is a beautiful sight to behold.

bred dogs—should be bred. Altered dogs, however, can participate in other AKC events such as obedience trials and the Canine Good Citizen program.

Before you actually step into the ring, you would be well advised to sit back and observe the judge's ring procedure. If it is your first time in the ring, do not be over-anxious and run to the front of the line. The judge asks each handler to "stack" the dog, hopefully showing the dog off to his best advantage. The judge will observe the dog from a distance and from different angles, and approach the dog to check his teeth, overall structure, alertness and muscle tone, as well as consider how well the dog "conforms" to the standard. Most importantly, the judge will have the exhibitor move the dog around the ring in some pattern that he should specify (always

Yorkies are quite a hit in the show ring, with their flowing coats, groomed to perfection, and their sparkling confidence and showmanship.

INFORMATION ON CLUBS

You can get information about dog shows from the national kennel clubs:

American Kennel Club
5580 Centerview Dr., Raleigh, NC 27606-3390
www.akc.org

United Kennel Club
100 E. Kilgore Road, Kalamazoo, MI 49002
www.ukcdogs.com

Canadian Kennel Club
89 Skyway Ave., Suite 100, Etobicoke, Ontario
M9W 6R4 Canada
www.ckc.ca

The Kennel Club
1-5 Clarges St., Piccadilly, London W1Y 8AB, UK
www.the-kennel-club.org.uk

listen since some judges change their directions—and the judge is always right!). Finally, the judge will give the dog one last look before moving on to the next exhibitor.

If you are not in the top four in your class at your first show, do not be discouraged. Be patient and consistent, and you may eventually find yourself in a winning line-up. Remember that the winners were once in your shoes and have devoted many hours and much money to earn the placement. If you find that your dog is losing every time and never getting a nod, it may be time to consider a different dog sport or to just enjoy your Yorkshire Terrier as a pet. Parent clubs offer other events, such as agility, tracking, obedience, instinct tests and more, which may be of interest to the owner of a well-trained Yorkshire Terrier.

OBEDIENCE TRIALS

Obedience trials in the U.S. trace back to the early 1930s when organized obedience training was developed to demonstrate how well dog and owner could work together. The pioneer of obedience trials is Mrs. Helen Whitehouse Walker, a Standard Poodle fancier, who designed a series of exercises after the Associated Sheep, Police Army Dog Society of Great Britain. Since the early days, obedience trials have

SHOW QUALITY SHOWS
While you may purchase a puppy in the hope of having a successful career in the show ring, it is impossible to tell, at eight to ten weeks of age, whether your dog will be a contender. Some promising pups end up with minor to serious faults that prevent them from taking home an award, but this certainly does not mean they can't be the best of companions for you and your family. To find out if your potential show dog is show-quality, enter him in a match to see how a judge evaluates him. You may also take him back to your breeder as he matures to see what he might advise.

grown by leaps and bounds, and today there are over 2,000 trials held in the U.S. every year, with more than 100,000 dogs competing. Any registered AKC dog can enter an obedience trial, regardless of conformational disqualifications or neutering.

Obedience trials are divided into three levels of progressive difficulty. At the first level, the

Yorkies are groomed to the last minute before being presented to the judge. The patient Yorkie endures the primping right up until his turn in the ring.

The Yorkshire puppy can grow to become the adult that the owner chooses. Given exposure to proper training and experience, your Yorkie can become a star show dog or an agility master.

able points in each exercise; the possible points range from 20 to 40 for each exercise.

Each level consists of a different set of exercises. In the Novice level, the dog must heel on and off leash, come, long sit, long down and stand for examination. These skills are the basic ones required for a well-behaved "Companion Dog." The Open level requires that the dog perform the same exercises above but without a leash for extended lengths of time, as well as retrieve a dumbbell, broad jump and drop on recall. In the Utility level, dogs must perform ten difficult exercises, including scent discrimination, hand signals for basic commands, directed jump and directed retrieve.

Once a dog has earned the UD title, he can compete with other proven obedience dogs for the coveted title of Utility Dog Excellent (UDX), which requires that the dog win "legs" in ten shows. Utility Dogs who earn "legs" in Open B and Utility B earn points toward their Obedience Trial Champion title. In 1977, the title Obedience Trial Champion (OTCh.) was established by the AKC. To become an OTCh., a dog needs to earn 100 points, which requires three first places in Open B and Utility under three different judges.

The Grand Prix of obedience

Novice, dogs compete for the title Companion Dog (CD); at the intermediate level, the Open, dogs compete for the title Companion Dog Excellent (CDX); and at the advanced level, dogs compete for the title Utility Dog (UD). Classes are sub-divided into "A" (for beginners) and "B" (for more experienced handlers). A perfect score at any level is 200, and a dog must score 170 or better to earn a "leg," of which three are needed to earn the title. To earn points, the dog must score more than 50% of the avail-

trials, the AKC National Obedience Invitational gives qualifying Utility Dogs the chance to win the newest and highest title: National Obedience Champion (NOC). Only the top 25 ranked obedience dogs, plus any dog ranked in the top 3 in his breed, are allowed to compete.

AGILITY TRIALS

Having had its origins in the U.K. back in 1977, AKC agility had its official beginning in the U.S. in August 1994, when the first licensed agility trials were held. The AKC allows all registered breeds (including Miscellaneous Class breeds) to participate, providing the dog is 12 months of age or older. Agility is designed so that the handler demonstrates how well the dog can work at his side. The handler directs his dog over an obstacle course that includes jumps as well as tires, the dog walk, weave poles, pipe tunnels, collapsed tunnels, etc. While working his way through the course, the dog must keep one eye and ear on the handler and the rest of his body on the course. The handler gives verbal and hand signals to guide the dog through the course.

The first organization to promote agility trials in the U.S. was the United States Dog Agility Association, Inc. (USDAA), which was established in 1986 and spawned numerous member

MEET THE AKC
The American Kennel Club is the main governing body of the dog sport in the United States. Founded in 1884, the AKC consists of 500 or more independent dog clubs plus 4,500 affiliate clubs, all of which follow the AKC rules and regulations. Additionally, the AKC maintains a registry for pure-bred dogs in the U.S. and works to preserve the integrity of the sport and its continuation in the country. Over 1,000,000 dogs are registered each year, representing about 150 recognized breeds. There are over 15,000 competitive events held annually for which over 2,000,000 dogs enter to participate. Dogs compete to earn over 40 different titles, from Champion to Companion Dog to Master Agility Champion.

clubs around the country. Both the USDAA and the AKC offer titles to winning dogs. Three titles are available through the USDAA: Agility Dog (AD), Advanced Agility Dog (AAD) and Master Agility Dog (MAD). The AKC offers Novice Agility (NA), Open Agility (OA), Agility Excellent (AX) and Master Agility Excellent (MX). Beyond these four AKC titles, dogs can win additional ones in "jumper" classes, Jumpers with Weave

Obedient,
glamorous and
intelligent—is it
possible that the
Yorkshire Terrier
has it all?

Novice (NAJ), Open (OAJ) and Excellent (MXJ), which lead to the ultimate title(s): MACH, Master Agility Champion. Dogs can continue to add number designations to the MACH titles, indicating how many times the dog has met the MACH requirements, such as MACH1, MACH2, and so on.

Agility is great fun for dog and owner, with many rewards for everyone involved. Interested owners should join a training club that has obstacles and experienced agility handlers who can introduce you and your dog to

---

FIVE CLASSES AT SHOWS

At most AKC all-breed shows, there are five regular classes offered: Puppy, Novice, Bred by Exhibitor, American-bred and Open. The Puppy Class is usually divided as 6 to 9-months of age and 9 to 12-months of age. When deciding in which class to enter your dog, male or female, you must carefully check the show schedule to make sure that you have selected the right class. Depending on the age of the dog, its previous first-place wins and the sex of the dog, you must make the best choice. It is possible to enter a one-year-old dog who has not won sufficient first places in any of the non-Puppy Classes, though the competition is more intense the further you progress from the Puppy Class.

---

the "ropes" (and tires, tunnels and the rest).

TRACKING

Any dog is capable of tracking, using his nose to follow a trail. Tracking tests are exciting and competitive ways to test your Yorkshire Terrier's instinctive scenting ability. The AKC started tracking tests in 1937, when the first AKC-licensed test took place as part of the Utility level at an obedience trial. Ten years later in 1947, the AKC offered the first title, Tracking Dog (TD). It was not until 1980 that the AKC added the Tracking Dog Excellent title (TDX), which was followed by the Versatile Surface Tracking title (VST) in 1995. The title Champion Tracker (CT) is awarded to a dog who has earned all three titles.

In the beginning level of tracking, the owner follows the dog through a field on a long leash. To earn the TD title, the dog must follow a track laid by a human 30 to 120 minutes prior. The track is about 500 yards long with up to five directional changes. The TDX requires that the dog follow a track that is three to five hours old over a course up to 1,000 yards long with up to seven directional changes. The VST requires that the dog follow a track up to five hours old through an urban setting.

INDEX

My Yorkshire Terrier

PUT YOUR PUPPY'S FIRST PICTURE HERE

Dog's Name _____

Date _____ Photographer _____